COLORFUL
CROCHET
KNITWEAR

SANDRA GUTIERREZ

DAVID & CHARLES

www.davidandcharles.com

CONTENTS

INTRODUCTION

To me, the materials in a crochet pattern often read like the ingredients in a potion: some yarn and a hook; all that you need to make magic happen. Many people think that crochet is limited—and sometimes crochet garments may feel too "craftsy" to wear—but with my designs I often hear people say "I had no idea you could make that with crochet!". I want to show the world that crochet knitwear is just as versatile as knitted garments, if not more so, and can be just as professional-looking. I also want to show how crochet colorwork techniques open infinite doors of self-expression and fun with yarn!

This book is designed to teach you my favorite colorwork techniques, including tapestry, mosaic, intarsia and stripes—with all of their variations and interpretations. Each technique section includes a detailed explanation and a small swatch lesson for you to practice the technique on a small scale. It also includes sections on how to choose the right colors and fibers for your project, as well as important tips for making garments. The last section includes not only basic crochet stitches, but also techniques that I love using in my garments. If you need extra help understanding any of these techniques, feel free to visit my website at NomadStitches.com for extra guidance.

Color has been a language for me since I was a little girl. Subtlety has never been my strength, and since becoming a knitwear designer I have truly loved discovering new ways of mixing colors while creating professional-looking garments that people can wear in their everyday lives.

As an adult, I have lived in ten different countries, and my love of languages and foreign cultures almost matches my love of yarn. One thing that I have learned on my travels is that clothes are more than just something you wear to keep warm. They are a way to express who we are and how we feel. Handmade garments in particular have the magic of carrying with them memories and emotions of the time you spent making them. They are like a language. In that spirit, I have been inspired to name each one of the designs after beautiful words that don't have direct translations into English.

Once you have gained confidence in the techniques and you are ready to make knitwear, I invite you to dive into the fourteen new patterns contained in this book. They are designed to showcase the versatility of crochet and motivate you to learn something new. They have modern, uncomplicated shaping that will flatter anybody and will keep you entertained while making them. Every one of the designs represents something beautiful and has become, at one time or another, my favorite. I made them all while pregnant with my second daughter, so they have even more significance for me. I really hope you like them as much as I do and that you have fun planning the color palettes for each of them.

Happy Crocheting!

COLOR THEORY

Color has been my greatest ally since I was a little girl. I am not always the most outgoing person, but I always want my clothes and accessories to do the screaming for me. I clearly remember my obsession over my neon pink shorts and my bright purple backpack. Ever since then, I knew that color was a way of expressing myself. Now, as an adult and a knitwear designer, color is one of my greatest tools. With it, I reflect on the inspiration behind garments and usually try to convey a feeling. So yes, color is more of an intuitive thing to me. However, color theory is a science and it would be remiss of me to write a book about crochet colorwork and not talk about the science behind picking harmonious colors for your project.

Choosing the best colors

Here are some tips to make the best choices so that the garments you make are garments you love and, more importantly, wear.

THE COLOR WHEEL

Let's go back to elementary school and study the color wheel for a second. Here, you will find your primary colors (red, blue and yellow), secondary colors (the ones made by combining primary colors) and tertiary colors (those that are made by combining secondary colors with primary colors).

Here are other terms you might want to know when talking about color:

Hue: Any color in the color wheel.

Shade: The shade of a color can be altered by adding black to any hue, making it deeper and richer.

Tint: A tint is created by adding white to a hue, making it lighter and less intense.

Tones: Tones are altered by adding gray to any hue, creating a more subtle version of the same color.

Saturation: The purity of a color.

Luminance: The brightness of a specific color.

Using the color wheel is the most science-based way to pick colors. If you find it hard to visualize these combinations on paper, just head to an internet browser and search for "color wheel palette generator" and you will find lots of tools to help you make the matching easier.

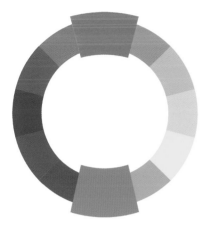

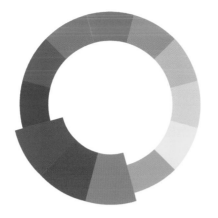

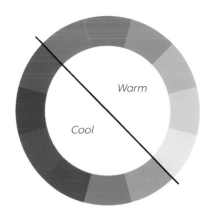

Complementary colors

When using two colors, you can simply use complementary colors, which are any two colors directly opposite each other in the color wheel. They have the highest contrast, but can look a bit garish, so be careful. In my Commuovere pullover, I used yellow and blue, which are complementary colors.

Analogous colors

These are any three colors that sit together in the color wheel. This often makes the color scheme much less intense than some of the other combinations, but it can still be very pleasing to the eye.

Warm or cool colors

The wheel can be split into warm and cool colors. According to psychologists who study color, different temperatures can evoke different feelings. For example, cool colors are linked to serenity and isolation, while warm colors make you think of coziness and warmth.

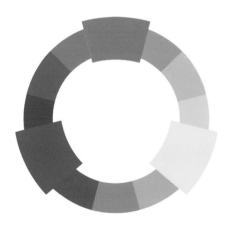

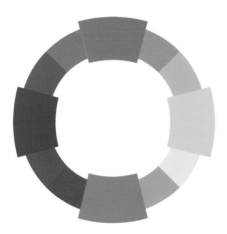

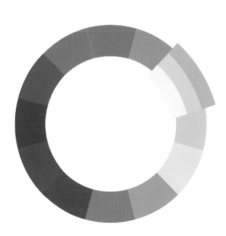

Triadic colors

When using three colors, you can use triadic colors, which are in any three evenly spaced points around the wheel. They will have less contrast than complementary colors, but also create a very bright palette. You can observe this in the Lagom pullover.

Tetradic colors

When using four colors, use tetradic colors, which are in any four evenly spaced points in the wheel. However, keep in mind that the more colors you have in your palette, the harder they are to harmonize. The Pana Po'o summer top is a good example of how to balance tetradic colors.

Work within one hue

Another easy way to pick colors is to stick to one hue and pick different shades, tints and tones. It will not be the boldest of combinations, but you can be safe in knowing that it will work and it will be harmonious.

NEUTRAL COLORS

These don't show up in the color wheel; they include beige, gray, ivory, browns, black and white. Because of their lack of color, they are great when mixed with color. So when in doubt, match your favorite color or color combination with your favorite neutral for a winning palette. I do this a lot, as seen in the Hygge jacket, the Commuovere pullover or the Lagom pullover.

FIND INSPIRATION IN NATURE

You know that saying, "Nature knows best"? Well, it really is true. Some of the most harmonious combinations I have used have come straight from nature. If it looks good in a picture, why not on a jumper? So next time you're looking for inspiration for a project, head to your garden or browse the internet for nature shots and stick to the palette of those images. My Ailyak pullover combination came straight out of my garden!

DO THE GRAYSCALE TEST

Sometimes you think you have a winning combination because the colors fall in the right place on the color wheel, or one is a neutral. However, the level of contrast between two colors depends not only on hue, but also on tint, shade and saturation. The easiest way to find out if two colors have enough contrast when worked together is to take a picture of them and convert it to grayscale. If the grayscale image shows the colors to be almost identical, the contrast won't be strong. If they show as two contrasting grays, the colors will pop. Sometimes a subtle contrast is desirable, but usually the higher the contrast the more a motif will stand out.

SWATCH

The best way to work out if a color combination will be a winner is simply to make a swatch. Sometimes what looks good on paper simply doesn't feel right when worked up as crochet in your actual chosen yarns. Swatching also helps determine if your choice of fiber is the best one for the project—see Getting Started: Yarn for examples of how different fibers can affect the colorwork result. So save yourself future disappointment by taking the time to swatch before you begin on the actual project. You have no idea how many times I have restarted or regretted entire garments because I wasn't happy with the way the colors worked together. Learn from my mistakes and swatch!

HAVE FUN

Last, but definitely not least, remember that color is a way of self-expression, so have fun with it! Do you feel like using neon colors? Do it! If you're a bit scared of looking too clown-like in such bright colors, pair them up with something a little more muted, like a neutral color. For the Commuovere pullover and the Ailyak pullover, I knew I wanted the yellow and the pink to really stand out and be super intense, but by using brown with the zingy yellow and a tweedy green with the bright pink, the neon effect doesn't feel like too much; it feels just right. So really try out some options and have fun!

Photo by Ilja Frei on Unsplash

GETTING STARTED

Crocheting garments is not just about having crochet skills. There is so much information to learn about the best tools and materials for each job. Also, reading patterns might feel like a minefield if you have never done it before. This chapter will introduce you to the basics of reading a crochet pattern and the different tools and materials you will need. There is also advice on choosing substitute materials when the ones listed are not available. I hope this chapter will help you will feel more prepared to tackle all of the projects in this book and many more.

Hooks

Crochet hooks are the most important tool for crocheting and they come in lots of shapes and sizes: there are flashy ones with lots of colors and cool handles, and there are also really basic ones. They are usually made of wood, aluminum, acrylic, plastic or bamboo. Although they are all great, they are not all equal. Try out a few kinds of hook to find your favorite, and get a complete set of those. There is very little you can't make with a set of hooks from US size B/1 to N/15 (2.00 to 10.00mm)—it's also the most affordable way to stock up!

Parts of a hook

The hook is made up mostly of a handle and head. The handle gives you stability when working and, depending on your grip, some handles will be more comfortable than others. My favorite type of hook has an aluminium head and a plastic handle. The head is made up of the throat, tip and lip. The circumference of the throat determines the size of the crochet hook. This is where loops rest while working stitches. Both the tip and lip can be used to get into stitches, although the tip is the most used. Rounded but pointy is the ideal shape for both.

Hook size conversion chart

Depending on where you are in the world, crochet hooks will be measured differently. Here's a little table to help you understand the different classifications, although each pattern gives the suggested hook size in both US and metric.

METRIC	US	UK
2.00mm	–	14
2.25mm	B/1	13
2.50mm	–	12
2.75mm	C/2	11
3.00mm	–	11
3.25mm	D/3	10
3.50mm	E/4	9
3.75mm	F/5	-
4.00mm	G/6	8
4.50mm	-	7
5.00mm	H/8	6
5.50mm	I/9	5
6.00mm	J/10	4
6.50mm	K/10.5	3
7.00mm	–	2
8.00mm	L/11	0
9.00mm	M/13	00
10.00mm	N/15	000

Tip Head Handle

Lip

Throat

Yarn

Although you can crochet with anything that is string-like (wire, fairy lights, rope, twine...), yarn is the most popular material for crocheting and comes in all sorts of sizes, fibers and colors. Some of the most common fibers are wool, acrylic and cotton. Other natural fibers that are widely used include flax, linen, bamboo, silk, mohair, alpaca and cashmere. There are advantages and disadvantages to each kind of fiber and, depending on what you're making, it's important to make the right choice. When choosing yarn, it is important to know what you are making and to touch, feel and try the yarn out.

WOOL

Wool is wonderful! It is breathable and has waterproofing properties, it keeps odors away and can be incredibly warm. It also has a lot of memory, which means that garments won't stretch and stay stretched, but will usually return to their original shape. When it comes to price, wool ranges from quite cheap to quite expensive, depending on the treatment it has had, its provenance and if it's been machine or hand dyed. Wool is also a great option for colorwork since it expands beautifully and fills the gaps between stitches, while still keeping good stitch definition. It can sometimes be a bit itchy and rough, although the roughness is what draws many into loving wool. The down side is that it usually requires a lot of care when washing to avoid felting. A good solution to both these issues is Superwash Wool, which goes through a chemical treatment that makes it softer and machine washable. However, the wonderful rustic element of wool is sometimes lost after going through this treatment.

COTTON AND LINEN

Cotton and linen share many properties. They are both plant-based and neither is very elastic, which means they tend to relax in the direction of gravity; they have excellent drape but not much memory. Cotton is often used for accessories, home decor or blankets, but both cotton and linen are known for their breathability during hotter months—unlike wool, they can move heat away from your skin. Cotton and linen are both good options for colorwork but not always the best: their good stitch definition sometimes means it's too easy to distinguish between stitches, instead of seeing the motif as a whole.

ACRYLIC

Acrylic yarn is a man-made fiber that comes from petroleum products. It gets a bad rep (let's be honest, it's not my favorite), but has a lot of good points. It's cheap, lightweight, easy to care for, and is very soft, strong and durable. However, it doesn't breathe like natural fibers and can create low quality work due to lack of structure and stitch definition (especially cheaper brands).

BLENDS

Blends mix different fibers to combine their properties. For example, sock yarn of wool and acrylic nylon is very sturdy so will make durable socks that are warm, soft and breathable. Combining cotton and acrylic softens cotton fibers and improves memory while keeping breathability and making garments wearable in hot weather. The same goes for cotton-wool blends. Both these blends will usually be much lighter than 100% cotton yarn.

Wool swatch

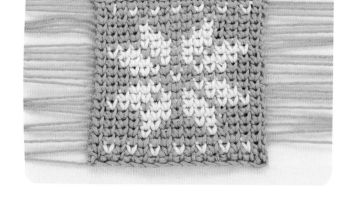

Cotton swatch

FUZZY YARN

Some fibers tend to be quite fuzzy, such as mohair and alpaca. These can be a bit tricky to work with as it can be hard to distinguish the exact place you need to work into on each stitch, but the results are usually wonderfully soft. These types of fibers are not the best option for colorwork since the fuzziness creates a halo that takes away stitch definition. However, that same halo might be used as a feature to elevate a colorwork motif and make it more interesting.

HAND-DYED YARNS

Over the last few years the availability and popularity of hand-dyed yarn has grown immensely. This type of yarn is usually much more expensive than that sold by big-box stores because it must be dyed in small batches and is usually of high-quality natural materials like merino wool, cashmere and silk. The colorways that dyers are able to create with this method are usually very striking and beautiful. They often mix several colors and, depending on the technique used, the effect changes: they can be speckled, tonal, variegated, kettle-dyed, hand-painted or ombre. The fact that one single skein of yarn combines different colors adds a level of challenge to using hand-dyed yarn in a colorwork project. A good idea when using this type of yarn is to stick with colorways that are predominantly of a single color (speckled or tonal) as I did in the Forelsket shawl and Ailyak pullover; or to match them with a solid color for maximum contrast, as in the Merak hat and cowl.

YARN WEIGHTS

Yarn weight refers to the thickness; thinner yarn is lighter weight and thicker yarn is heavier—for more information, search online for the Craft Yarn Council's system of classification. Each pattern gives the weight of yarn used; garments tend to be made in size 1 to 5, but most of my garments are made using size 1 (fingering or 2–3ply) or 2 (sport or 3–4ply), which are considered lightweight. Here are some pros and cons to working with lightweight yarn:

Pros

- You can get much more detail in a smaller area, so it's great for texture, colorwork and lace.

- It makes for a lighter fabric with more drape—in my opinion, this means more wearable crochet garments.

- Skeins usually have more yarn in them, so you might feel like you are making a thriftier choice.

Cons

- It often takes longer to finish a project.

- If you have never used lightweight yarn, it may feel odd and will take time to adjust to smaller hooks and yarn.

- It could potentially make the fabric very thin and not as warm if using a hook that is too large.

Most yarn comes with suggested hook sizes on the label. These are recommendations and not what you must use since different combinations of yarn and hook create different fabrics. A big hook with lightweight yarn will create a light, drapey fabric that can be a bit open. A smaller hook with heavier yarn will create tighter stitches without any holes, but also a heavier and bulkier fabric.

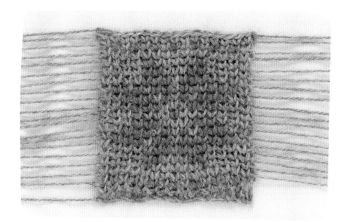

Mohair swatch

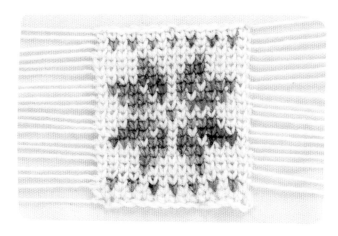

Hand-dyed swatch

SUBSTITUTING YARN

Designers usually take everything into consideration when designing a garment and will choose the best combination of fibers, yarn weight and hook size. However, it is not always possible for makers to obtain the same yarn as the one used in a pattern, so yarn substitutions are necessary.

What to keep in mind when substituting yarn

1. Try to use a similar fiber to the one in the pattern—a light summery cardigan designed with a bamboo/cotton blend will look very different if you make it with wool.

2. Make sure you obtain the gauge (tension) listed in the pattern with your chosen yarn and that you are happy with the fabric created. If the fabric doesn't feel right (too open or heavy), it might be a good idea to consider a different option.

Gauge (tension)

Gauge is one of the most overlooked sections of a pattern, but it is an integral part of making a garment that fits. If your gauge doesn't match the gauge in the pattern, your finished garment will be bigger or smaller than intended. Gauge measures how big stitches are. It is usually measured in stitches and rows over a 4 x 4in (10 x 10cm) square. Most professional patterns include a gauge measurement since this is the measurement the designer used to make sure the garment is the correct size. To measure the gauge, first make a gauge swatch: a square of fabric to test your chosen yarn with a hook that you think will approximate the intended gauge. I recommend making a square at least 6 x 6in (15 x 15cm). So, for example, if the gauge in a pattern is 18 sts x 15 rows = 4 x 4in (10 x 10cm), make a square that is at least 27 sts x 23 rows. Count how many stitches and rows fit in 4 x 4in (10 x 10cm) in the middle of the square. If you have more than 18 sts in then your stitches are too small and you need to try again with a bigger hook. If you have fewer than 18 sts then your stitches are too big and you need to try again with a smaller hook.

Sometimes you will achieve the right gauge on the first try, other times it will take you a few goes. However, I cannot help but insist on the importance of this step. Even when you are using the same yarn used in the pattern, tension varies from person to person, and it is so important that you use the right hook size to achieve the intended finished measurements.

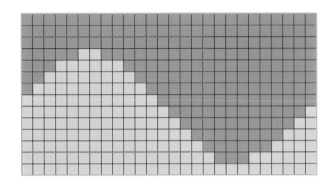

KEY

☐ Worsted (aran) weight swatch

☐ Fingering (2ply) weight swatch

The chart shows the different area of the design covered in swatches made the same size but using different weights of yarn.

Swatch of chart section worked in worsted (aran) yarn

Swatch of chart section worked in fingering (2 to 3ply) yarn

Blocking

It is also imperative to block both your gauge swatch and your finished project.

Blocking is a process in which the fibers relax and take on new sizes and shapes. When blocking, stitches will expand and the material will usually grow. Blocking can also be used to keep edges straight and to open up a lace pattern. If you obtain gauge with an unblocked swatch and make a garment using that gauge, at the moment of blocking your garment, the size of it will change. Some of my favorite blocking techniques include steaming, wet blocking and spray blocking.

To block an item, pin it out to the correct size and shape. The method you then choose will depend to some extent on what is best for the yarn fiber. To steam block, use a steam iron set to steam held just above the surface—do not actually touch the item with the iron. To wet block, the item must be completely immersed in water before you pin it out. To spray block, spray the item thoroughly after it is pinned out. After any of these methods, leave the item pinned in place until it is completely dry.

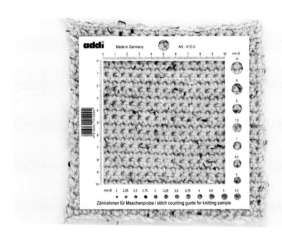

A gauge swatch before blocking

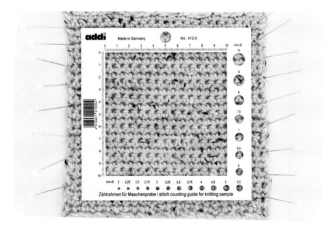

A gauge swatch after blocking

Abbreviations

There are two main abbreviation systems: US and UK. I use only US abbreviations in the patterns in this book. See General Techniques: Abbreviations for a list of the most common abbreviations used in this book, followed by a US/UK crochet terms conversion table. Some special stitches with their abbreviations are listed at the beginning of the relevant pattern.

Sizes and measurements

Choosing the correct size for a project can be tricky, but it is important to make the right choice at the start because not all sizes are the same in a pattern nor can they all easily be modified later. For all my patterns I give the finished garment measurements (see Project Information) and it is up to the maker to decide which size will fit them best.

Another thing to be aware of is ease, which refers to the difference between an actual body measurement and the garment. Negative ease means that the garment is smaller than your body, which comes in handy for stretchy, fitted garments. When a garment has positive ease it is larger than your actual body measurements, so the garment will be loose. The more positive ease there is, the looser the garment will be. When choosing a size and considering ease, measure your body and add the amount of ease suggested, or subtract negative ease. Then choose the closest size to that number. For example, my bust measures 39½in (100cm). If a garment was designed with 4in (10cm) of positive ease, I will choose the size that is closest to 43½in (110cm) around the bust. However, ease is just a design element that the designer uses to grade a pattern with an intended look; for instance, if they want a loose summer tank top to be loose. So it's a good idea to consider the intended ease of a pattern when choosing a size—for example, if you would like an oversized garment pick a larger size. If you are not a fan of loose garments, then go smaller. A good tip is to simply measure your favorite sweater or t-shirt and make the size that is closest to that one.

Colorwork techniques

TAPESTRY CROCHET

Tapestry is probably the most heard of and used crochet colorwork technique—and many use this term inaccurately to refer to any colorwork. As its name suggests, it was first developed to make tapestries, such as rugs or home décor items. However, it is a very versatile technique that can be used to decorate anything from accessories to garments. People are often put off because they compare it to stranded knitting, and the motifs created with tapestry crochet can sometimes seem lacking, but I have found that changing the stitches used can make a big difference to the way a motif looks and tapestry crochet garments can easily compete with knitted ones.

Tapestry crochet basics

The idea behind tapestry crochet is to use more than one color of yarn per row, making color changes within a row to create motifs, and carrying the unused yarn on the inside of the stitches ready to be used whenever it is needed. Most of the time you will follow a color chart, which makes it very easy to count stitches and to visualize the image you are working on. Although you can use as many colors as you want per row, I find that using more than two can become a bit too difficult to manage and makes your fabric heavier. However, it is certainly possible to use as many colors as your heart desires on every row. Traditionally, tapestry crochet is worked with single crochet, but it can also be done with double crochet or with variations of single crochet. Overall, tapestry crochet is a wonderful technique. I have used it for many of my patterns and, while the process might seem slower and at times more complicated, I firmly believe that the extra struggle is worth it for a stunning garment that is wearable art. I hope you do too!

Single crochet flat

Using single crochet and working in flat rows (where you come and go, turning at the end of every row) is an effective way of working tapestry; but is not my favorite. Crochet stitches look very different front and back, so the difference between rows is noticeable and motifs can be distorted. This method is usually better for very simple motifs over larger surfaces. There are two great advantages to this way of working tapestry crochet: the first is that it's the only variation with single crochet that is worked flat (think blankets or scarves), which means you don't have to work in circles. The other advantage is that the right side and wrong side will look the same.

Single crochet in the round

Working single crochet in circular rounds with every row facing the right side helps a lot in the definition of motifs, but it does bring up a new issue. When you work single crochet rounds the stitches tend to lean, and this makes motifs look a bit slanted. The image might be clearer, but it is still not my favorite way of working tapestry crochet.

Single crochet flat

Single crochet in the round

Single crochet variations

Here are some modified versions of single crochet that create the best motif definition and help stitches align straight instead of leaning sideways. All of these modifications are worked on the right side only, which means that they must be worked in circular rounds. Alternatively, you must cut your yarn at the end of every row and go back to the beginning for the following row.

SINGLE CROCHET BACK LOOP ONLY (SCBLO)

Working in the round with scBLO fixes the leaning issue that existed with plain single crochet rounds. To make a scBLO, you work regular single crochet but instead of inserting your hook into both loops of a stitch, you work only on the back loop. For an example of this in a garment, see the Iktsuarpok tank top.

CENTRAL SINGLE CROCHET (CSC)

This stitch, which is also known as waistcoat stitch, is one of my favorite ways of working tapestry crochet. I sometimes call it Fair Isle crochet because of how much the look of it closely resembles knitting Fair Isle. When this stitch is worked in the round, the stitches perfectly align on top of each other as you work round upon round. Also, because of the way the stitches are worked, each one looks like a little "V", which emulates a knit stitch—giving you great definition. To work in central single crochet, you must first work one base round of single crochet, then work the following rounds using central single crochet (see General Techniques: Central Single Crochet). It can be a bit tricky the first few times you try it and is hardest at the beginning of your work, but it does get easier.

A neat trick that I have learned is to use the lip of the hook, not the tip, to enter the stitch. This helps open up the path for the hook. Also, keeping stitches loose is incredibly important to be able to enter stitches in between that "V". If you are a tight crocheter this might feel completely unnatural and you will have to train your hands to keep the stitches loose to avoid frustration. Another thing to keep in mind is that the fabric can sometimes become quite thick, so it is a good idea to use lighter weight yarn and a bigger hook. In my Commuovere pullover pattern, I used fingering weight yarn with a US size H/8 (5mm) hook to achieve a lightweight fabric with clear motifs.

EXTENDED SINGLE CROCHET (ESC)

Motifs created with this stitch will tend to be a little bit elongated since the stitch is slightly longer than a regular single crochet, single crochet BLO or central single crochet. However, stitch definition is really good, stitches align on top of each other and they don't lean. Overall, I would say this is a winning technique (see General Techniques: Extended Single Crochet for how to work it). You can practice it making Ailyak pullover in the Projects section of this book.

Single crochet back loop only

Central single crochet

Extended single crochet

Techniques

There are some rules that apply to all variations of tapestry crochet.

COLOR CHANGES

Color changes happen on the stitch prior to the one with a new color; the idea is to finish that stitch with the new color so that it can then be used to work the following stitch. So the final yarn over when finishing a stitch must be done with the new color.

Color change with single crochet: insert the hook in the stitch (where you insert it will depend on whether you are working sc, scBLO, or csc), yo and pull through the stitch, drop the old color and pick up the new color (1), yo and pull through the remaining loops on the hook. (2)

Color change with extended single crochet: insert the hook in the stitch, yo and pull through the stitch, yo and pull through one loop on hook (3), drop the old color and pick up the new color, yo and pull through the remaining loops on the hook. (4)

Color change at the end of a row when working flat: change color on the last stitch to start the next row with the new color before the 1 chain at the beginning of the row.

Color change at end of a round: finish the last st in the old color, on the joining slip stitch insert the hook in the first st of the round and pull through the new color (5), dropping the old color, 1 ch to start the next round with the new color. (6)

Color change at end of a round with invisible join: slip stitch with the old color, pull to tighten the slip stitch, make the turning chain by yo with the new color and pull through (7), pull the old color to tighten the 1 ch (8). This method is my favorite because it is less complicated. And since the join remains invisible, the sts keep their color integrity throughout.

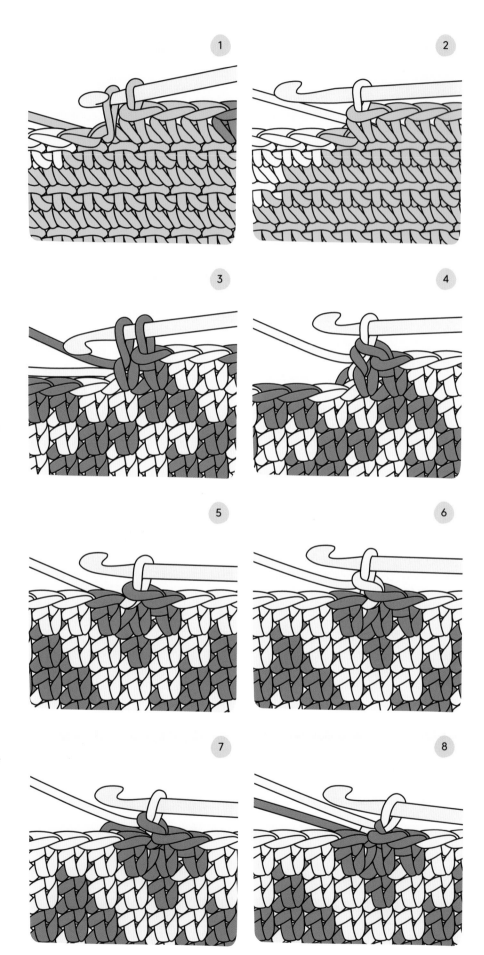

CARRYING FLOATS

When you are working tapestry crochet you will always have one or more colors that are not being used that you need to carry along until the next time the chart calls for them. They are called floats. The best way to keep your work neat and to hide your floats is to tuck the unused strands into the stitches as you work them: insert the hook in the stitch as directed, placing the unused strands of yarn on top of the hook (9), yo and work the stitch as normal with the working strand of yarn, keeping the unused strands on the inside of your stitch (10).

Make sure that the floats are not being pulled too tight to avoid scrunching up your work and to keep some elasticity in your fabric—you might want to pull on your work slightly before using the next color, especially if the float is particularly long (5 or more stitches).

Sometimes there are rows with only one color. If you are working flat, determine if you will be able to reach your unused yarn on the following row to decide if you should carry it along or not. For example, if there are two rows in which Yarn B is not needed, you can leave it at the beginning of the row and when you return after the two rows, it will be there for you to use. However, if there is only one row in which Yarn B is not used you must carry it along so that it is available for you to use when you turn your work for the following row. If you are working in rounds you don't have to worry about this; you can simply leave behind any colors that are not used to avoid having to worry about carrying floats.

Depending on the yarn and stitch being used, sometimes it's possible to see floats on the right side. If this happens, turn your work to face the wrong side and pull on the float that is peeking through with a small hook. Your wrong side will look less neat, but the right side will thank you.

Let's swatch

Make a chain that is multiples of the chart (in this case, multiples of 12). If you are working in rounds, slip stitch in first chain to join. On every round to follow, 1 ch at the beginning of the round (it never counts as a st) and slip stitch in the first st of the round to join. If you are working flat, make sure to 1 ch at the beginning of every row (doesn't count as a st).

Follow the chart provided using whatever variation of the technique you would like to practice: this is the same chart used in all of the swatches in this chapter.

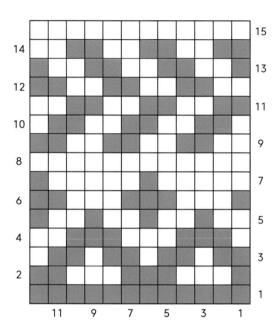

KEY

☐ A ▨ B

Read the chart from the bottom up.

Each square represents one sc stitch.

If working in rows, read from right to left on right side (odd-number) rows and from left to right on wrong side (even-number) rows.

If working in rounds, work from right to left on each round.

9

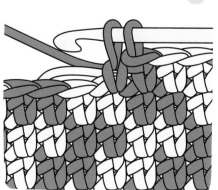

10

MOSAIC CROCHET

In the many years that I have been crocheting, mosaic crochet has been the one technique that I immediately fell in love with and haven't stopped using. It was created as an adaptation of mosaic knitting to make geometric motifs in a simple yet effective way. It is much simpler than other colorwork techniques, mainly because it requires you to only work with one strand of yarn at a time! The mosaic effect really is striking and the color and pattern possibilities are endless.

Charts

The easiest way to read a mosaic crochet motif is by using charts. They indicate what color to use on each row, and when to work short stitches (single crochet or chain) and long stitches (double crochet two rows down). The charts used for mosaic crochet look exactly the same as mosaic knitting charts. However, to make them easier to read, there is an X wherever long stitches are required.

There are two main mosaic crochet techniques and the charts are read differently in each. However, here are the basics that apply to both techniques:

- Each square in the chart represents one stitch.

- The first square of each row indicates the color that will be used throughout that row. Colors alternate on every row of the chart. So if the first square of a row is dark, only the color assigned to dark squares will be used on that row. The following row on the chart will be light and only the color assigned to the light squares will be used on that row.

- When a square is of the same color as the row, AND the square directly BELOW it is also of the same color, an X is used to indicate the need for a long stitch. So if a gray square on a gray row has another gray square directly below it will have an X. (A)

- Most mosaic crochet charts will include the X, but if they don't, it is best to mark them yourself before starting in order to make your work easier.

- Repeats are marked with vertical lines that run one or two stitches in from the edges of the chart. (B)

- Edge stitches need to be worked at the beginning and end of each row, but only the stitches between the lines will be repeated across the row.

- When working in the round, simply omit the stitches on the outside of the repeat lines and work in multiples of the stitches between the lines.

- When necessary my charts always include a Row 0, which is an extension of the foundation (see Let's Swatch)—you need Row 0 to work dropped stitches into on Row 1. If chart rows are worked again above the first repeat, then Row 0 will be omitted. Some charts form bands of pattern within a larger piece, in which case there is already a row beneath to work dropped stitches into, so Row 0 is not needed.

- You may come across a chart with Xs on Row 1 that doesn't have a Row 0 or previous plain rows to work them into. In this case, the simplest option is to copy the top row of the chart at the bottom of the chart as a Row 0, omitting any Xs. (C)

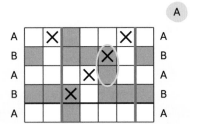

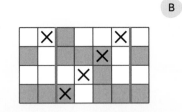

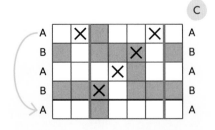

Techniques

It is often thought that mosaic crochet is a single technique, but people have developed it in different ways and I have found two main variations. I have named them to keep them separate in this book and in my teaching, although most people just call them both mosaic crochet. It is generally up to the reader and maker to decipher which technique the writer is referring to.

STANDARD MOSAIC CROCHET

This variation is the most commonly used. Each row of a chart corresponds to two rows on your work, which means it can be worked flat or in rounds. This also means that motifs will sometimes be slightly elongated. A great advantage of this technique is that the fabric doesn't gain any extra thickness and it won't develop any holes or gaps. At the same time, the way the motifs are worked creates great color definition.

There are three main stitches used in standard mosaic crochet:

1. Single Crochet: a sc is worked on any square that is the same color as the color of the row. So on a gray row, a gray square represents a sc.

2. Chain: a ch is worked on any square that is a different color to the color of the row. So on a white row, a gray square represents a ch.

   Whenever a chain is worked, the stitch below is skipped so as to not add any extra stitches to the stitch count.

3. Mosaic Double Crochet: A mdc is a double crochet worked into a stitch directly below and two rows down, on the previous row of the same color as the current one. (D, E)

   It is worked on any square with an X. If there are no Xs on the chart, it is worked in squares of the same color as the row, where the square directly BELOW is also the same color. So if on a white row a white square has a white square directly below, it represents a mdc.

   All mdc are only worked on the right side of the work and only on the indicated stitch.

   The stitch from the previous row behind a mdc will be skipped to avoid adding extra stitches to the stitch count.

   On wrong side rows, all mdc are replaced by sc.

Each row is read first from right to left on the right side (RS), then from left to right on the wrong side (WS). However, since the WS is a repeat of the RS, it is easy to simply "read" the previous row and make a sc on every sc or mdc stitch and a ch where a ch was previously made.

Some charts have motifs that create bands or pictures, beginning at the bottom and ending at the top. (F)

Others can be worked as many times as desired by repeating the chart over and over again. (G)

When working a chart such as the latter, it is necessary to "close" your work when it is time to stop repeating the chart. To do this, replace ALL CHAINS with sc on the RS and WS of the desired last row of the chart. After this you may work another chart or simply finish.

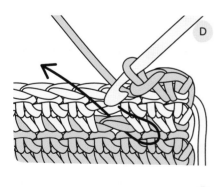

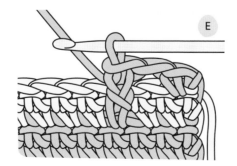

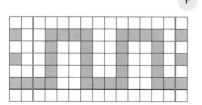

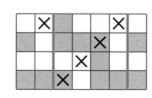

Changing color at the end of the row

The rows in a chart alternate in color. To change color and keep the edge as clean as possible when working flat, work as follows, starting on the last stitch of each WS row:

Insert the hook into the stitch, yarn over (yo) and pull through the stitch. (H)

Drop the old color and pick up the new color, yo and pull through 2 loops on the hook. (I)

Twist the old color around the new color to trap it in place. (J)

Then 1 ch with the new color. (K)

Turn. On the first stitch, hide the old color on the inside of the stitch as if carrying a float as follows: insert the hook into the stitch, place the old color yarn on top of the hook at the back of your work. (L)

Yo with the new color and pull through the stitch, yo and pull through 2 loops on the hook. (M)

Leave the old color where it is to pick up and work the following row. Continue working the rest of the row with the new color.

SINGLE-ROW MOSAIC CROCHET

This variation is much simpler that the standard version. Each row of the chart corresponds to each row of work, which means that is it better worked in rounds. Although it can be worked in flat rows, each strand of yarn must be cut at the end of every row since it needs to always be worked on the right side. Unlike standard mosaic crochet, single-row creates a thicker fabric with some added texture and, although color definition sometimes suffers from this, the effect created is still very special.

There are only two stitches used in this variation of mosaic crochet:

1. Single Crochet in the Back Loop Only: a scBLO is worked on ANY square, regardless of color, that doesn't have an X in it.

2. Double Crochet in the Front Loop Only: a dcFLO is worked two rows down on the previous row of the same color as the current row, on any square with an X in it. (N)

An X is only placed on a square of the same color as the row, where the square directly below it is also of the same color.

The stitch from the previous row behind a dcFLO will be skipped, which is to avoid adding extra stitches to the stitch count.

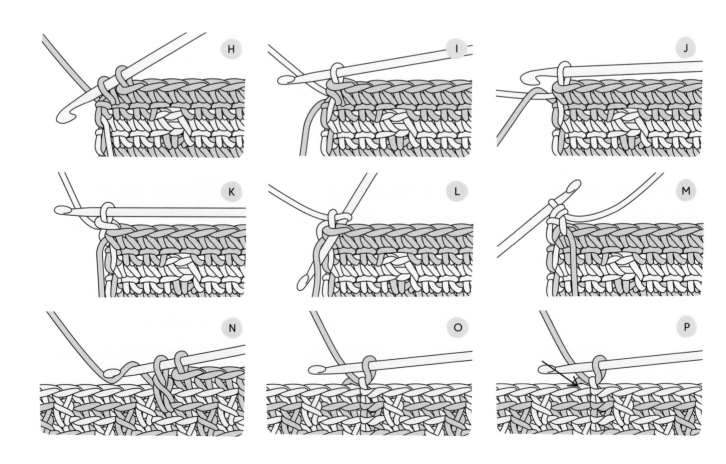

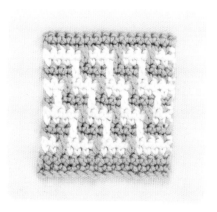

Standard mosaic crochet right side

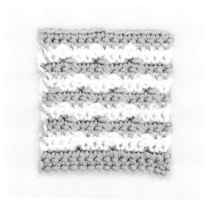

Standard mosaic crochet wrong side

Single-row mosaic crochet right side

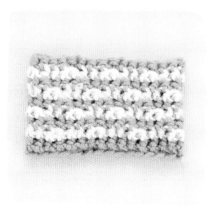

Single-row mosaic crochet wrong side

Changing color at the end of the round

Since single-row mosaic crochet is mostly worked in the round, I recommend using the invisible join technique (see General Techniques).

In order to change colors innocuously, slst on the first st of the round to join the round with the old color, then ch 1 with the new color. (O)

Make sure NOT to skip the first stitch. (P)

Continue with the following row using the new color.

Let's swatch

A foundation needs to be established before starting to follow a chart. For better color definition, the foundation is made in the opposite color to the first row of the chart. For standard mosaic crochet, this foundation starts with a long chain of as many stitches as necessary, then two rows of sc. For single-row mosaic crochet, you also start with a long chain joined to work in the round, and then one round of sc.

These swatches have both been worked from the same chart, but using different mosaic crochet techniques.

The wrong side of the fabric should only show stripes.

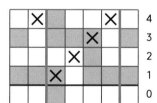

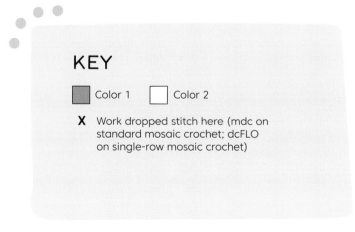

KEY

■ Color 1   □ Color 2

X Work dropped stitch here (mdc on standard mosaic crochet; dcFLO on single-row mosaic crochet)

INTARSIA CROCHET

Intarsia is one of those techniques that people often think it is difficult. However, in my experience, it is one of the easiest techniques and there are many advantages to using it; you can literally "draw" anything—all you need is a chart and different colored yarn. With intarsia, you make many different color sections in a row without having to carry the yarn along. You only work with one color at a time and when it's time to use a different color, you drop the old color, pick up the new one and go. The biggest disadvantage is that each section of color requires a separate live strand of yarn. This means that if a row has six sections of color you will need six separate strands of yarn. Working with so many strands can seem stressful, but there are a few techniques to make things easier, such as knowing how to manage yarn and make effective color changes.

Managing yarn

To avoid frustration, make sure your yarn is organized and ready to go before starting. I recommend placing the yarn balls in a basket arranged in the order in which they will be used on a row. When you turn your work, turn the basket to keep tangles to a minimum. Or, leave the basket in place, but make sure that if you turned your work to the right once, next time you turn to the left, and so on. Your yarn WILL probably tangle but it won't necessarily KNOT, so try to relax and enjoy the chaos.

MAKING BOBBINS

You can use whole balls of yarn for each live strand, but if the section of color is small the yarn is managed more easily as bobbins. To judge the right length of yarn, count the stitches that need to be covered in that section, plus extra for a tail at the beginning and end. For example,

if a color portion is 4 sts wide and 10 sts high, there is a total of 40 sts in it (4 x 10 = 40). Two loose wraps around your hook measures approximately the same as one single crochet stitch made with that hook, so loosely wrap the yarn around your hook ten times to measure how much yarn you need for five stitches. Alternatively, work a small swatch of five stitches and measure the yarn used when pulled apart. Then multiply this amount by eight (5 x 8 = 40) to figure out the necessary length for 40 sts. Remember to add a little more for a tail at the beginning and end, then cut your yarn.

The easiest way to make a bobbin is by wrapping the yarn around two fingers, leaving a small gap in between them (1). Then wrap the loops with the yarn end by passing the tail in between your fingers and making a very loose, temporary knot (2). Start working with the end from the beginning of the bobbin.

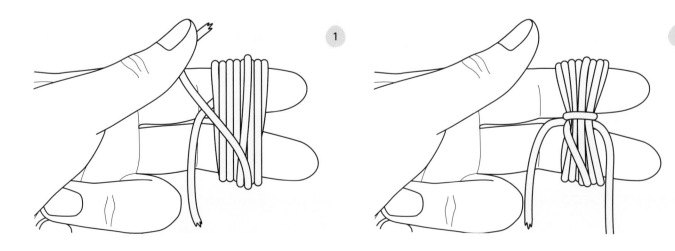

1

2

Techniques

You can work intarsia with any stitch that you want. Usually the motifs and images are presented in charts, which makes it easier to visualize the pattern you are making, but you sometimes also find written instructions. Whenever a new color is introduced on a row, you add a new live strand of yarn in that color. Once a section of a color is finished, cut the yarn and leave a tail to weave in later. Intarsia is mostly worked flat, but there is no reason not to work it in the round. The only thing that you must do is turn your work at the end of every round.

COLOR CHANGES

Color changes always happen on the stitch prior to the one with a new color; the idea is to finish that stitch with the new color so the following stitch can be worked with that color. This will look different for different stitches, but here are some of the most common color changes that will give you an idea of the technique.

Color change with single crochet: insert the hook in the stitch, yo and pull through the stitch, drop the old color and pick up the new color, yo and pull through the remaining loops on the hook. (3)

Color change with double crochet: yo, insert the hook in the stitch, yo and pull through the stitch, yo and pull through 2 loops on the hook, drop the old color and pick up the new color, yo and pull through the remaining loops on the hook.

Color change on a chain: drop the old color and pull through the new color to make a chain. Note that on the next row, when working on the starting chain, as you pick up a new strand the last chain of that color will tighten—make sure NOT to skip any chains to keep your stitch count correct. (4)

Color change at end of a row: make the color change on the last yo of the very last st to start the following row with the new color.

Color change in middle of row with slip stitch: place the old color at the back of the work on RS rows or pull toward the front of the work underneath the hook on WS rows, insert the hook in the stitch, yo in the new color, pull through the stitch and the loop on the hook.

Color change in middle of row with double slip stitch: yo, insert the hook in the stitch, place the old color at the back of the work on RS rows or pull toward the front underneath the hook on WS rows, yo in the new color, pull through the stitch and the loops on the hook.

3

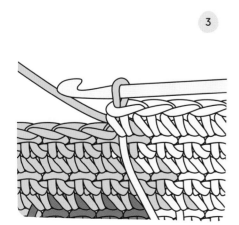

4

WRONG SIDE VS RIGHT SIDE

Another advantage of intarsia crochet is that the wrong and right sides are almost identical—but they are not interchangeable. To keep the right side neat and tidy, always keep the live strands of yarn on the wrong side of your work during a color change. So when working on the right side, leave the yarn at the back of your work when changing color. When working on a wrong side row, at the moment of dropping the old yarn you need to place it in front of your work going under your hook (5)—this process is less intuitive since you have to force the yarn from its usual resting place at the back of your work.

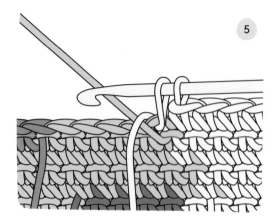

Let's swatch

When starting an intarsia project that has sections of different colors on the first row, I recommend changing colors on the starting chain to match. Then follow the chart until completion.

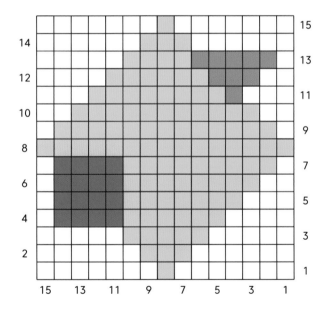

Intarsia swatch right side

Intarsia swatch wrong side

KEY

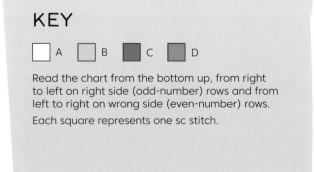

☐ A   ☐ B   ■ C   ■ D

Read the chart from the bottom up, from right to left on right side (odd-number) rows and from left to right on wrong side (even-number) rows.

Each square represents one sc stitch.

STRIPES AND COLORBLOCKING

Using stripes or colorblocking is a very effective way of adding personality and accents to a design. Incredibly easy to do, it is the perfect way to introduce yourself to colorwork techniques, and there is not much prep needed so improvisation is very simple.

Stripes

The effects created vary depending on the color contrast involved, and the width and frequency of the stripes. You can be bold or subtle, decorative or strategic; you can use stripes to blend colors together—and they are great for using up scraps!

BOLD STRIPES

If you want a big statement, using high contrast colors with evenly-spaced stripes will do the job; in the Jayus cardigan, the black and white sleeves definitely pop. Other high contrast combinations will also be effective at adding drama to your garment.

SUBTLE STRIPES

To tone things down but still add personality, thin stripes are the best way to go. You can alternate thin stripes with thick stripes, or keep them all the same narrow width. The use of color is also very important—if you combine cream and light pink, the effect will be much more subtle than if you mix black and neon yellow.

Colorblocking

Colorblocking means making large portions in one color—the body of the Jayus cardigan is a perfect example. This technique is easy and, depending on the colors, the effect can be bold or subtle. In garments, color blocks can help accentuate parts of your body that you like and help blend in bits you want to play down. As a rule of thumb, bright colors will catch the eye, while neutral tones avoid attention—so to accentuate your hips because you have broad shoulders, for example, use a neutral color on top with darker or brighter colors below.

FADE

To create a faded or ombre effect, use colors that are similar or contain elements of each other—this is very easy with hand-dyed yarn or non-solid colors. For example, you can more easily transition from green yarn with purple speckles to purple yarn with green speckles, than from solid green to solid purple. Another technique is to double strand two colors and transition with one while keeping the other the same. To create a faded effect, start with thick stripes of the original color and thin stripes of the new color, then make stripes the same width, and finally thinner stripes of the original color and thicker of the new. The longer the transition, the subtler it will be—see Let's swatch or the Forelsket shawl.

Techniques

Here are some useful techniques when working with stripes or colorblocking.

COLOR CHANGES

See Colorwork Techniques: Tapestry Crochet section for how to work color changes at the end of a row when working stripes or colorblocking flat or in the round.

CUT OR CARRY

If the stripes are not too far apart, you can carry the yarn along the edge (if working flat) or at the join (if working in rounds). To do this, you must tack in the unused strands to avoid having a big loop of yarn where a color wasn't used.

Tack in the round

The easiest method is to wrap the unused yarn inside the slip stitch that you make to join the round: insert your hook in the first stitch of the round, place the unused strand on top of your hook (1), yo with the working yarn and pull through the stitch and remaining loop on the hook (2), then work your turning chain. This keeps the unused strand nicely tucked in at the back of your work behind the join and ready to use when you need it next.

Tack when flat

When working stripes flat, you will always have a visible edge that the unused strands must travel up. If the stripes are wide and you don't want to have the yarn visible on the side of your work, it's best to cut your yarn and weave in the ends later on. However, if the stripes are narrow enough, you can tack the yarn along to keep it neat and avoid having long loops: simply twist your unused strand of yarn around your working yarn at the end of the row before (3) and after the turning chain (4). This will move the yarn along as you work, to be ready when it is needed next. Pull on the unused strand a little bit to make it taut against the edge and avoid any loops.

Odd or even

Another thing to consider when deciding to cut or carry your yarn is whether the stripes are an odd or even number of rows. When working in the round it doesn't make a difference since the beginning of every round is in the same place. But when working flat, stripes with an odd number of rows will start and finish in a different place. Since crochet stitches look very different when viewed from the front than the back, I recommend you always cut your yarn at the end of an odd row and attach the next color for the following row. This will add to the ends you need to weave in later, but it will keep the stitch pattern undisturbed.

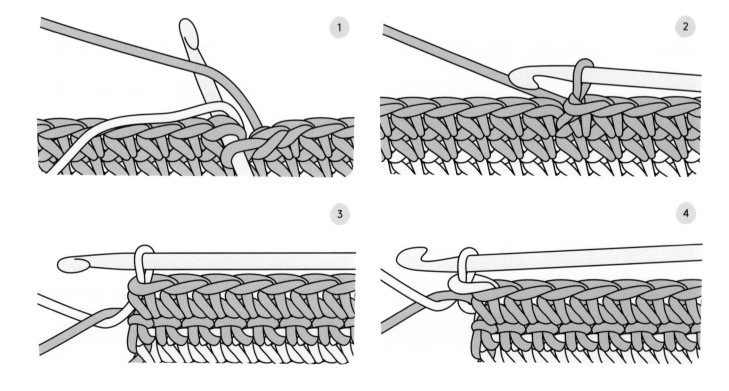

Let's swatch

Stripe patterns are not always presented as charts, but some are. Here, the instructions are in both written and charted form. Decide if you are working in rounds or flat, then keep in mind the width of the stripes (odd or even) and practice tacking the unused yarn as you go.

PATTERN

Work in A until start of transition.

1 row with B

3 rows with A

1 row with B

2 rows with A

1 row with B

2 rows with A

2 rows with B

2 rows with A

2 rows with B

1 row with A

2 rows with B

1 row with A

3 rows with B

1 row with A

Cont with B only.

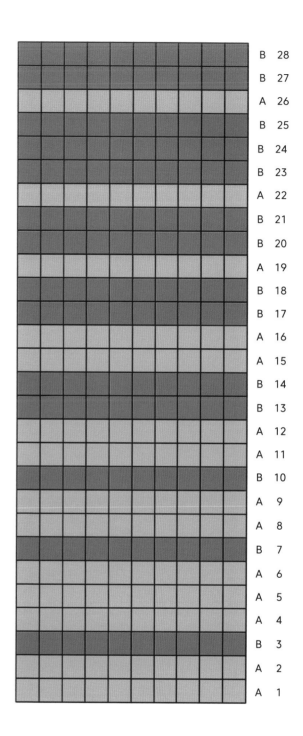

B	28
B	27
A	26
B	25
B	24
B	23
A	22
B	21
B	20
A	19
B	18
B	17
A	16
A	15
B	14
B	13
A	12
A	11
B	10
A	9
A	8
B	7
A	6
A	5
A	4
B	3
A	2
A	1

KEY

A   B

Each stitch represents one sc.
Don't forget to ch1 at the beginning of every row/round.

The projects

Wabi Sabi hat and mittens

Wabi Sabi (Japanese) — refers to the thought or world view of finding beauty in nature's imperfections.

See Project Information for finished size dimensions.

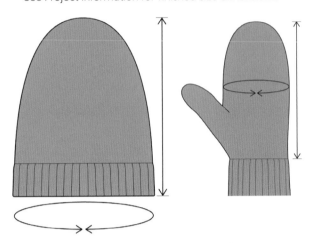

SIZES

Hat: 3 sizes (S, M, L)
Mittens: 2 sizes (M, L)

YARN

Rosa Pomar Mondim (100% Portuguese wool), fingering (2ply), 100g (421yd/385m), in the following colors:

HAT

A: Heather Lichen (305); ½ (½, ½) ball
B: Dark Blue (113); ¼ (¼, ¼) ball
C: Rose (110); ¼ (¼, ½) ball

MITTENS

A: Heather Lichen (305); ¼ (½) ball
B: Dark Blue (113); ¼ (¼) ball
C: Rose (110); ¼ (¼) ball

TOOLS

US size H/8 (5mm) hook
2 stitch markers

GAUGE (TENSION)

18 sts x 24 rows = 4 x 4in (10 x 10cm) over waistcoat stitch in the round using a US size H/8 hook.

SPECIAL ABBREVIATIONS

csc, central single crochet (waistcoat stitch): insert hook in the middle of V and under top loop, yo, pull up a loop, pull through both loops on hook

The motifs in these mittens and hat represent nature—leaves growing in spring and water rippling; two everyday occurrence that are full of beauty. They are meant to remind you to look for the good even when it's hard to see. Both the hat and mittens are worked in tapestry crochet using waistcoat stitch, which gives them a knitted look.

NOTES

The hat is made bottom-up, first working the brim vertically in slip stitch ribbing. Keep stitches loose so you will be able to work into them and to keep the elasticity of the ribbing—use a larger hook for this if necessary. The body of the hat is worked in waistcoat stitch in rounds to the crown, following the chart. The stitches left at the crown are woven together and the opening closed.

The mittens are also worked bottom-up, starting at the ribbed cuffs. The hand is worked from a chart on the top side and stripes on the inside, increasing at one side for the thumb. The rest of the hand is worked in rounds following the same pattern of stripes on the inside and chart on the back. When the desired length is reached, the top is worked, decreasing at each side, and the opening is closed. Finally, the thumb is finished in a striped pattern.

Hat

BRIM

Using A, ch 18.

Row 1: Skip first ch, slst in each ch, turn. 17 sts

Row 2: 1 ch, slstBLO to end of row, turn. 17 sts

Rep prev row for a total of 100 (110, 120) rows.

On WS, slst tog FLO of last worked row and starting ch. Turn work inside out to work on side edge of ribbing on RS.

BODY

Note: keep sts loose and use invisible join throughout (see General Techniques).

Set-up round: 1 ch, sc along side edge of ribbing, fitting 1 st on side of every row of ribbing, slst in first st to join. 100 (110, 120) sts

Beg working in central single crochet (csc).

Change to B and cont foll Hat chart using B and C, rep it 10 (11, 12) times around. Do not cut A, carry it on the inside ready to use again by tacking inside slsts when joining each round.

To add length, rep any portion of Hat chart before decreases as necessary.

At the end of chart there will be 20 (22, 24) sts.

Last round: 1 ch, csc2tog around, slst to join. 10 (11, 12) sts

Fasten off, leaving a long tail to close gap at top.

Using a tapestry needle, weave the tail into each stitch around. Pull tightly to close opening and fasten off on inside.

Hat chart

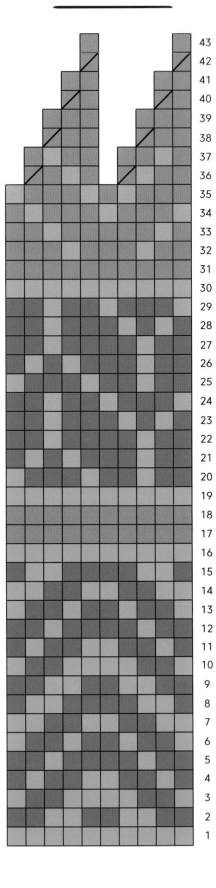

KEY

■ A   ■ B   ▢ C   ◩ csc2tog decrease

Read the chart from bottom to top, right to left.

Rep each row around, making 1 ch at beg of round and using invisible join to join (see General Techniques, Invisible Join When Working in Rounds).

Each square represents one stitch.

Mittens

CUFF

Note: keep sts very loose.

Using A, ch 18.

Row 1: Skip first ch, slst in each ch, turn. 17 sts

Row 2: 1 ch, slstBLO to end of row, turn. 17 sts

Rep prev row for a total of 33 (39) rows.

On WS, slst tog FLO of last worked row and starting ch. Turn work inside out to work on side edge of ribbing on RS.

HAND

Note: keep sts loose and use invisible join throughout.

Set-up round: 1 ch, sc along side edge of ribbing, fitting 1 st on side of every row of ribbing, slst in first st to join. 33 (39) sts

Cont with Right or Left hand.

RIGHT HAND

Work in central single crochet (csc) throughout. Carry A on inside ready to use again by wrapping it inside slsts when joining round.

Round 1: 1 ch, follow Mittens chart 1 for first 16 (19) sts of round, using B, csc and PM in next st, 16 (19) cscs, slst to join. 33 (39) sts

Note: remember to carry unused yarn along last part of row (see Tapestry Crochet: Carrying Floats). Ch 1 at beg of round (does not count as a st) and use invisible join throughout.

Round 2: Foll Mittens chart 1 to before marker, 3 csc in marked st (PM in first and third st of last 3 sts), using C, csc to end of round, slst to join. 35 (41) sts

Round 3: Foll Mittens chart 1 to before marker, using B, csc to end of round, move all markers up, slst to join. 35 (41) sts

Round 4: Foll Mittens chart 1 to before marker, inc1 in marked st, PM in first st of inc, csc to before next marker, inc1 in marked st, PM in second st of inc, using C, csc to end of round, slst to join. 37 (43) sts

Rep Rounds 3 and 4 another 4 (5) times. 45 (53) sts

Rep Round 3 twice more, without inc. 45 (55) sts

Thumb-separating round: Using B (do not carry C), 1 ch, csc to before marker, 1 ch, skip 13(15) sts of thumb until second marker, csc to end of round, slst to join, remove markers. 33 (39) sts incl 1 ch where thumb was

REST OF HAND

Set-up round: Using A (do not carry other yarns), 16 (20) csc, csc and PM in next st, csc to end of round, slst to join—work on ch made to close off thumb as any other st. 33 (39) sts

Round 1: Foll Mittens chart 2 to before marker, using C, csc to end of round, slst to join, move marker up on every round.

Round 2: Foll Mittens chart 2 to before marker, using B, csc to end of round, slst to join.

Rep Rounds 1 and 2 another 8 (9) more times.

Skip ahead to Rounded Top.

KEY

 B   C

Read the chart from bottom to top, right to left.

Rep each row around, making 1 ch at beg of round and using invisible join to join (see General Techniques, Invisible Join When Working in Rounds).

Each square represents one stitch.

Work only the section inside the red lines indicated for your size.

*Rows 1 and 16 are for the L size only.

Mittens chart 1

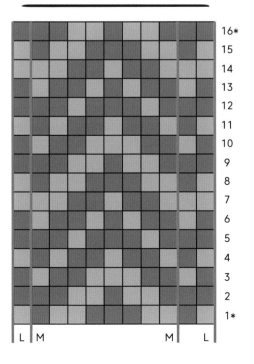

LEFT HAND

Work in central single crochet (csc) throughout.

Round 1: Change to B, 1 ch, 16 (19) csc, csc and PM in next st, foll Mittens chart 1 in last 16 (19) sts of round, slst to join. 33 (39) sts

From now on, carry both B and C along first portion of round to use them on chart.

Round 2: Using C, 1 ch, csc to before marker, 3 csc in marked st (PM in first and third st of last 3 sts), foll Mittens chart 1 to end of round, slst to join. 35 (41) sts

Round 3: Using B, 1 ch, csc to second marker, move both markers up, foll Mittens chart 1 to end of round, slst to join. 35 (41) sts

Round 4: Using C, 1 ch, csc to before marker, inc1 in marked st, PM in first st of inc, csc to before next marker, inc1 in marked st, PM in second st of inc, foll Mittens chart 1 to end of round, slst to join. 37 (43) sts

Rep Rounds 3 and 4 another 4 (5) times. 45 (53) sts

Rep Round 3 twice more, without inc. 45 (53) sts

Thumb-separating round: Using B (do not carry C), 1 ch, csc to before marker, 1 ch, skip 13(15) sts of thumb until second marker, csc to end of round, slst to join, remove markers. 33 (39) sts incl 1 ch where thumb was

REST OF HAND

Set-up round: Using A (do not carry other yarns), 16 (18) csc, csc and PM in next st, csc to end of round, slst to join. 33 (39) sts

Round 1: Using C, 1 ch, csc to marker, foll Mittens chart 2 to end of round, slst to join.

Round 2: Using B, 1 ch, csc to marker, foll Mittens chart 2 to end of round, slst to join.

Rep Rounds 1 and 2 another 8 (9) times.

Cont with Rounded Top.

ROUNDED TOP

Change to A, cut other yarns and remove marker.

Round 1: 1 ch, csc to last 2 sts—PM in 16th (19th) st)—csc2tog, slst to join. 32 (38) sts

Round 2: 1 ch, 1 csc, csc2tog, csc to 3 sts before marker, csc2tog, csc and PM in next st, csc in next st, csc2tog, csc to last 3 sts, csc2tog, csc in last st, sl st to join the round. 28 (34) sts

Round 3: 1 ch, csc around, move marker up, slst to join.

Rep Rounds 2 and 3 another 3 times. 16 (22) sts

Rep Round 2 once more. 12 (18) sts

Fasten off, leaving a long tail to close gap at top.

KEY

 B   C

Read the chart from bottom to top, right to left.

Rows 2 and 19 are for the L size only.

Rep each row around, making 1 ch at beg of round and using invisible join to join (see General Techniques, Invisible Join When Working in Rounds).

Each square represents one stitch.

Work only the section inside the red lines indicated for your size.

Mittens chart 2

| | | | | | | | | | | | | | | | | | | | | 20 |
| 19 |
| 18 |
| 17 |
| 16 |
| 15 |
| 14 |
| 13 |
| 12 |
| 11 |
| 10 |
| 9 |
| 8 |
| 7 |
| 6 |
| 5 |
| 4 |
| 3 |
| 2 |
| 1 |

L · M · · M · L

Turn each mitten inside out. Using mattress stitch, weave together first 6 (9) sts with last 6 (9) sts to close opening at top. Fasten off and weave in ends.

THUMB

On the RS, attach C to unused loop of chain at the thumb opening, next to the hand.

Round 1: 1ch, sc in st where yarn was attached, csc2tog in next 2 sts, csc around to last 2 sts, csc2tog, slst to join. 12 (14) sts

Change to B.

Csc around for a further 7 (8) rows, or until desired length of thumb, alternating color rows between C and B on every row and joining at the end of every round.

ROUNDED TOP

Change to A

Round 1: 1 ch, *1 csc, csc2tog in next 2 sts, rep from * around to last 0 (2) sts, csc in last 0 (2) sts, slst to join. 8 (10) sts

Round 2: 1 ch, csc around, slst to join. 8 (10) sts

Round 3: 1 ch, csc2tog around, slst to join. 4 (5) sts.

Fasten off and cut leaving a long tail to close the opening.

Turn mitten inside out and weave tail through each st around opening using a tapestry needle. Pull to tighten and close hole. Fasten off.

Repeat Thumb on the other mitten.

Finishing

Block to measurements.

Attach a pompom to the top of the hat if desired.

Commuovere pullover

Commuovere (Italian) — to be moved in a heartwarming way, usually relating to a story that moved you to tears.

See Project Information for finished size dimensions.

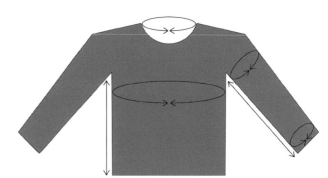

Commuovere is a romantic garment, one that tells a story of life and love. A striking piece with tapestry motifs that evoke true emotions, it is worked top-down, mostly in rounds. Its construction creates a comfortable fit around neckline and shoulders and means it's highly adaptable to all body shapes. The garment is worked in central single crochet (waistcoat stitch) for a knitted look and the fabric created is light yet warm, which makes it very wearable.

SIZES
9 sizes (1–9)

YARN
Knit Picks Palette (100% Peruvian wool) fingering (2ply), 50g (231yd/211m), in the following colors:
A: Marine Heather; 1¼ (1½, 1½, 1¾, 1¾) (2, 2, 2, 2¼) balls
B: Canary; 1¼ (1½, 1½, 1¾, 1¾) (2, 2, 2, 2¼) balls
C: Bison; 5 (5½, 6, 6½, 7) (7½, 7¾, 8¼, 8¾) balls

TOOLS
US size H/8 (5mm) hook
US size I/9 (5.5mm) hook
5 stitch markers

GAUGE (TENSION)
17 sts x 23 rows measure 4 x 4in (10 x 10cm) over csc (waistcoat st) colorwork using a US size H/8 (5mm) hook.

SPECIAL ABBREVIATIONS
csc, central single crochet (waistcoat stitch): insert hook in middle of V and under top loop, yo, pull up a loop, pull through both loops left on hook
csc2tog, decrease one stitch: *insert hook in middle V of next st, yo, pull through, rep from *, yo, pull through all loops on hook

NOTES

The pullover is worked top-down, starting at the slip stitch ribbed neckline—keep stitches loose so you can work into them and to keep the elasticity of the ribbing. Short rows are worked at the back of the neck for a better fit around neck and shoulders. The yoke is worked in circles using the chart and written instructions (see Colorwork Techniques: Tapestry Crochet), while at the same time increasing throughout. Once the yoke is complete, the body is separated from the sleeves and worked to the desired length, with another colorwork motif followed by a ribbed hem. The sleeves are then worked and finished with a ribbed cuff.

Use an invisible join (see General Techniques: Invisible Join When Working in Rounds) to join rounds throughout.

When working csc on the WS, the post of the stitches looks more like this "π" than a "v". Try to work stitches between the legs of the post under the top loops for a look that is as uniform as possible to csc in the round.

Main body

NECKLINE

Using US size I/9 and A, ch 11 (or as many ch as desired width of ribbing).

Row 1: Skip first ch, slst in each ch, turn. 10 sts

Row 2: 1 ch, slstBLO to end of row, turn. 10 sts

Rep Row 2 for a total of 90 (90, 96, 100, 100) (100, 104, 106, 110) rows or until ribbing measures approx 18½ (18½, 19⅞, 20⅞, 20⅞) (20⅞, 21⅝, 22¼, 23) in/47 (47, 50.5, 53, 53) (53, 55, 56.5, 58.5) cm WITHOUT much stretching, making sure it fits over your head and lays flat comfortably around the neck.

On WS, slst tog FLO of last worked row and starting ch. Turn work inside out to work on side edge of the ribbing on RS.

Set-up round: Using US size H/8 hook, sc around on side of ribbing making sure you have a total of 90 (90, 96, 100, 100) (100, 104, 106, 110) sts, slst in first st to join round.

Note: You may need to work one st every 2 rows of ribbing in places if you made more than the recommended number of rows. Remember to keep sts loose to start working in csc on foll round.

SHORT ROWS

Row 1 will go to one side, inc twice, turn; Row 2 will return to center of back without inc, then cont on to other side, inc twice, and turn. Row 3 will return to center of back again and close round. Use invisible join to join short row rounds; the join will run at center back.

There are 3 (3, 3, 4, 4) (4, 4, 4, 4) sets in total.

Cont in csc only.

Row 1 (RS): 1 ch (doesn't count as a st throughout), 1 csc in first st, PM to mark beg of round, 6 (6, 7, 6, 6) (6, 7, 7, 8) csc, 2 csc in next st, PM in first st of inc, 17 (17, 18, 17, 17) (17, 17, 18, 19) csc, 2 csc in next st, PM in second st of inc, 2 (2, 3, 3, 3) (3, 3, 3, 3) csc, turn. 30 (30, 33, 31, 31) (31, 32, 33, 35) sts

Row 2 (WS): 1 ch, skip first st, csc to beg of round moving all markers up, csc in beg of round and PM, 1 ch (doesn't count as a st), 6 (6, 7, 6, 6) (6, 7, 7, 8) csc, 2 csc in next st, PM in first st of inc, 17 (17, 18, 17, 17) (17, 17, 18, 19) csc, 2 csc in next st, PM in second st of inc, 2 (2, 3, 3, 3) (3, 3, 3, 3) csc, turn. 58 (58, 64, 60, 60) (60, 62, 64, 68) sts

Row 3 (RS): 1 ch, skip first st, csc to beg of round moving all markers up, slst in beg of round to join round. 28 (28, 31, 29, 29) (29, 30, 31, 33) sts

First set of short rows completed.

Row 4 (RS): 1 ch, csc in first st (beg of round) and PM, *csc to marker, 2 csc in marked st* and PM in first st of inc, rep from * to * and PM in second st of inc, csc to "step" left at end of prev short row, csc in "step", csc in next 3 sts of neck, turn. 35 (35, 38, 36, 36) (36, 37, 38, 40) sts

Row 5 (WS): 1 ch, skip first st, csc to beg of round moving all markers up, csc in beg of round and PM, 1 ch (doesn't count as a st), *csc to marker, 2 csc in marked st* and PM in first st of inc, rep from * to * and PM in second st of inc, csc to "step" left at end of prev short row, csc in "step", csc in next 3 sts of neck, turn. 68 (68, 74, 70, 70) (70, 72, 74, 78) sts

Row 6 (RS): 1 ch, skip first st, csc to beg of round moving all markers up, slst in beg of round to join round. 33 (33, 36, 34, 34) (34, 35, 36, 38) sts

Second set of short rows completed.

Rep Rows 4 to 6 another 1 (1, 1, 2, 2) (2, 2, 2, 2) times.

At this point, there are 38 (38, 41, 44, 44) (44, 45, 46, 48) sts at each side of beg of round st; a total of 102 (102, 108, 116, 116) (116, 120, 122, 126) sts around neck incl: 77 (77, 83, 89, 89) (89, 91, 93, 97) sts at Back, 2 short row steps, and 23 (23, 23, 25, 25) (25, 27, 27, 27) unworked neck sts at Front.

YOKE

Remove all markers. Start working in rounds on RS only. Inc Round 1 is the first to go around the whole neck; there are two inc rows on first portion of yoke before chart begins. Work on "steps" formed by short rows as on a normal st.

SIZE 1 ONLY

Inc round 1: 1 ch, [3 csc, inc1, 2 csc, inc1] 14 times to last 4 sts, 3 csc, inc1, slst in first st to join round. 131 sts – inc 29 sts

SIZES 2 (3) ONLY

Inc round 1: 1 ch, [2 csc, inc1] around, slst in first st to join round. 136 (144) sts – inc 34 (36) sts

SIZE 4 ONLY

Inc round 1: 1 ch, 2 csc, [2 csc, inc1] to last 3 sts, 3 csc, slst in first st to join round. 153 sts – inc 37 sts

SIZE 5 ONLY

Inc round 1: 1 ch, [1 csc, inc1, 2 csc, inc1] 22 times to last 6 sts, [1 csc, inc1] 3 times, slst in first st to join round. 163 sts – inc 47 sts

SIZE 6 ONLY

Inc round 1: 1 ch, [1 csc, inc1] to last 2 sts, 2 csc, slst in first st to join round. 173 sts – inc 57 sts

SIZE 7 ONLY

Inc round 1: 1 ch, inc1 in next 5 sts, [1 csc, inc1] 55 times to last 5 sts, inc1 in last 5 sts, slst in first st to join round. 185 sts – inc 65 sts

SIZE 8 ONLY

Inc round 1: 1 ch, inc1 in next 3 sts, [1 csc, inc1] twice, (inc1, 1 csc, inc1, 1 csc, inc1) 23 times, slst in first st to join round. 196 sts – inc 74 sts

SIZE 9 ONLY

Inc round 1: 1 ch, [inc1, 1 csc, inc1] 39 times to last 9 sts, inc1 in last 9 sts, slst in first st to join round. 213 sts – inc 87 sts

ALL SIZES

Next round: 1 ch, csc around, slst in first st to join round.

Rep prev round 3 (3, 3, 3, 3) (3, 4, 7, 9) more times

SIZE 1 ONLY

Inc round 2: 1 ch, [4 csc, inc1, 3 csc, inc1] 14 times to last 5 sts, 4 csc, inc1, slst in first st to join round. 160 sts – inc 29 sts

SIZES 2 (3) ONLY

Inc round 2: 1 ch, [3 csc, inc1] around, slst in first st to join round. 170 (180) sts – inc 34 (36) sts

SIZE 4 ONLY

Inc round 2: 1 ch, 2 csc, [3 csc, inc1] to last 3 sts, 3 csc, slst in first st to join round. 190 sts – inc 37 sts

SIZE 5 ONLY

Inc round 2: 1 ch, [2 csc, inc1, 3 csc, inc1] 22 times to last 9 sts, [2 csc, inc1] 3 times, slst in first st to join round. 210 sts – inc 47 sts

SIZE 6 ONLY

Inc round 2: 1 ch, [2 csc, inc1] to last 2 sts, 2 csc, slst in first st to join round. 230 sts – inc 57 sts

SIZE 7 ONLY

Inc round 2: 1 ch, [1 csc, inc1] 5 times, [2 csc, inc1] 55 times to last 10 sts, [1 csc, inc1] 5 times, slst in first st to join round. 250 sts – inc 65 sts

SIZE 8 ONLY

Inc round 2: 1 ch, [1 csc, inc1] 3 times, [2 csc, inc1] twice, [inc1, 2 csc, inc1, 2 csc, inc1, 1 sc] 23 times, slst in first st to join round. 270 sts – inc 74 sts

SIZE 9 ONLY

Inc round 2: 1 ch, [inc1, 2 csc, inc1, 1 csc] 39 times to last 18 sts, [1 csc, inc1] 9 times, slst in first st to join round. 300 sts – inc 87 sts

ALL SIZES

Cont working in csc and foll color Chart 1, rep each row a total of 16 (17, 18, 19, 21) (23, 25, 27, 30) times around. Cont to work 1 ch at beg of round, slst in first st to join round, and use invisible join technique.

SIZES 1 AND 2 ONLY

Move on to Body and Sleeves Separating Round after working Row 33. To add more rounds to yoke to lengthen for better fit, cont to foll chart to end then work rows of csc using C as necessary.

SIZES 3 TO 9 ONLY

Once chart is complete, work – (–, 1, 2, 7) (11, 13, 16, 19) rounds of plain csc using C. 224 (238, 252, 266, 294) (322, 350, 378, 420) sts

Chart 1

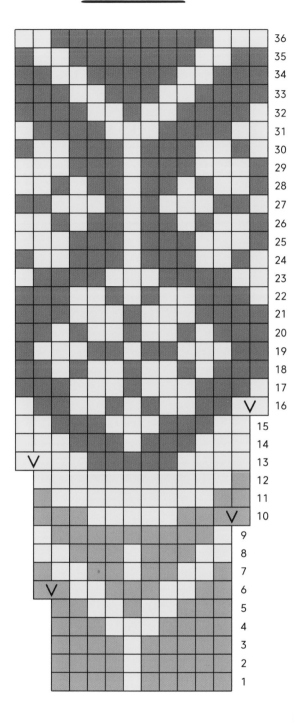

ALL SIZES

Note: Before working Separation Round, try on yoke and adjust length to desired measurements for a perfect fit. Add more rounds or remove some rounds of plain csc if desired.

Body and sleeves separation round: 1 ch, 32 (35, 38, 40, 42) (49, 52, 56, 64) csc (Back), 7 (8, 9, 11, 15) (15, 15, 15, 12) ch for first underarm, skip 49 (50, 51, 53, 57) (64, 71, 78, 82) sts (First Sleeve), 63 (69, 75, 81, 83) (97, 105, 111, 129) csc (Front), 7 (8, 9, 11, 15) (15, 15, 15, 12) ch for second underarm, skip 49 (50, 51, 53, 57) (64, 71, 78, 82) sts (Second Sleeve), csc to end of round, slst in first st to join round. 140 (154, 168, 182, 196) (224, 238, 252, 280) sts incl underarm ch

SIZES 1 AND 2 ONLY

If Chart 1 is not complete in Separation Round, cont to foll it when working Back and Front sts and make underarm ch using C. Carry B at underarm to cont using it later. For next 2 rows, or until Chart 1 is complete, rep chart around Body 10 (11) times, incl at underarm sts. Then fasten off B and cont using C only.

KEY

| | A | | B | | C | **V** 2 csc in same st (inc1) |

Read chart from bottom up and right to left. Each square represents one stitch worked in csc (waistcoat st).

Work 1 ch at beg of every round and use invisible join throughout (see General Techniques: Invisible Join When Working in Rounds).

Rep each row a total of 16 (17, 18, 19, 21) (23, 25, 27, 30) times around, omitting rows that don't correspond to chosen size.

Stitch count totals:

Rows 1 to 5: 160 (170, 180, 190, 210) (230, 250, 270, 300)

Rows 6 to 9: 176 (187, 198, 209, 231) (253, 275, 297, 330)

Rows 10 to 12: 192 (204, 216, 228, 252) (276, 300, 324, 360)

Rows 13 to 15: 208 (221, 234, 247, 273) (299, 325, 351, 390)

Row 16 onward: 224 (238, 252, 266, 294) (322, 350, 378, 420)

BODY

St count will remain constant throughout.

On next round, work csc on front and back sts, while working sc on underarm ch.

Cont in plain csc using C until Body is 9⅝ (10, 9½, 9¼, 8½) (8, 7¼, 6⅞, 6) in/24.5 (25.5, 24, 23.5, 21.5) (20, 18.5, 17.5, 15) cm from underarm, or until desired length from underarm minus 3⅜in (8.5cm) of Chart 2 and bottom hem.

Foll Chart 2 around, rep each row of chart 10 (11, 12, 13, 14) (16, 17, 18, 20) times around.

Once Chart 2 is complete, cont with Bottom Hem.

BOTTOM HEM

Using US size H/8 hook for tighter/ stretchier ribbing, ch 11.

Row 1: Beg in second ch from hook, slst to end of ch, when reaching body, skip very first st of round and slst in next st. 10 sts of ribbing

Row 2: Slst in next st, turn, skip 2 slsts done on body, slstBLO to end of row, turn. 10 sts

Row 3: 1 ch, slstBLO to end of row, slst in next empty st of body. 10 sts

Rep Rows 2 and 3 around bottom edge of body. On WS, join FLO of each st of last row of ribbing to each starting ch of ribbing with slsts.

Fasten off.

Sleeves

(work one in each sleeve opening)

Using US size H/8 hook, join C to middle of underarm to work on RS on unused loops of starting ch.

Set-up round: sc to end of underarm, csc around yoke sleeve sts, sc to end of round, slst in first st to join the round. Approx 56 (58, 60, 64, 72) (79, 86, 93, 94) sts

Notes: Work csc2tog in corners where underarm meets yoke to close any gaps if necessary.

If Chart 1 wasn't finished before Separation Round on sizes 1 and 2, foll chart on Yoke sts (starting where necessary to match what was done before) in Set-up Round and following rounds until Chart 1 is complete.

Work plain rows of csc for the next 2¾in (7 cm).

Dec round: 1 ch, csc2tog, csc around to last 2 sts, csc2tog, slst in first st to join round. 2 sts dec

Work 12 (7, 6, 5, 4) (3, 3, 2, 2) rounds of plain csc.

KEY

■ A □ B ■ C

Read chart from bottom up and right to left. Each square represents one stitch worked in csc (waistcoat st).

Work 1 ch at beg of every round and use invisible join throughout (see General Techniques: Invisible Join When Working in Rounds).

Chart 2

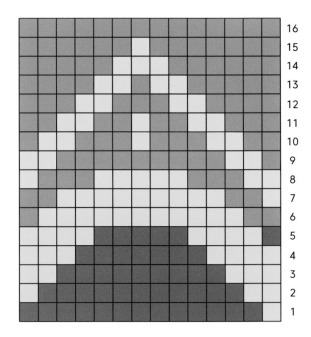

Rep Dec Round.

Cont shaping sleeves, working plain csc with a Dec Round every 13th (8th, 7th, 6th, 5th) (4th, 4th, 3rd, 3rd) round until desired sleeve circumference or until there are approx 10 (11, 12, 14, 17) (20, 23, 26, 26) Dec Rounds worked. Approx 20 (22, 24, 28, 34) (40, 46, 52, 52) dec sts

Work plain csc until sleeve is 14¾ (15⅛, 15⅛, 15¾, 15¾) (16⅛, 16⅛, 16¾, 16¾) in/37.5 (38.5, 38.5, 40, 40) (41, 41, 42.5, 42.5) cm from underarm, or desired sleeve length minus 1¾in (4.5cm) of ribbing.

CUFF

Rep ribbing as for bottom of body. Fasten off.

Finishing

Weave in all ends and block to measurements.

Iktsuarpok tank top

Iktsuarpok (Inuit) — the feeling of anticipation while waiting for someone to arrive, often leading to intermittently going outside to check for them.

See Project Information for finished size dimensions.

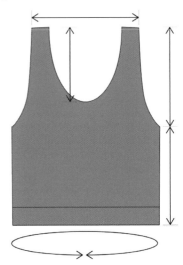

SIZES
9 sizes (1–9)

YARN
Knit Pick Swish DK (100% fine superwash merino), light worsted (DK), 50g (123yd/112m), in the following colors:

A: Nutmeg Heather; 1¼ (1¼, 1¼, 1½, 1¾) (1¾, 2, 2, 2¼) skeins

B: Moss; ½ (¾, ¾, ¾, 1) (1, 1, 1, 1¼) skeins

C: Amethyst Heather; 2¼ (2¼, 2½, 2¾, 3) (3¼, 3½, 3¾, 3¾) skeins

TOOLS
US size H/8 (5mm) hook

GAUGE (TENSION)
16 sts x 18 rows measure 4 x 4in (10 x 10cm) over single crochet worked flat using a US size H/8 (5mm) hook.

16 sts x 15 rows measure 4 x 4in (10 x 10cm) over single crochet back loop only worked in the round using a US size H/8 (5mm) hook.

The feeling of Iktsuarpok is something I am familiar with when waiting for spring, especially if the winter was particularly harsh or snowy. I spend most mornings during that time looking out the window in search of those first buds, and the Iktsuarpok tank is a taste of the beautiful feeling that comes when flowers start blooming, days get longer and the sun warms the earth. It's an easy project to introduce you to tapestry crochet and allow you to play with color.

NOTES

The top is worked bottom-up. The body is worked in rounds, following a color chart throughout (see Colorwork Techniques: Tapestry Crochet). Then the front and back are separated at the underarms and the panels are worked flat. The underarm is shaped while at the same time the neck is shaped at the front and back finishing in straps, which are then joined at the shoulders. An edging is worked around neckline and armhole openings to finish.

Body

Using A, make a crochet cord of 132 (144, 156, 180, 192) (204, 228, 240, 252) sts, slst in first st to join round.

From now on work on RS and in BLO only (incl on first row working in BLO of crochet cord sts) until otherwise stated.

Foll Chart rep each row 11 (12, 13, 15, 16) (17, 19, 20, 21) times around.

To add extra length, rep Chart Rows 13 to 24 or 13 to 36.

Fasten off A and B.

Next round (RS): Using C, 1 ch, scBLO around, slst to join round, turn.

Next round (WS): 1 ch, sc around, slst to join round.

FRONT

Before separating for underarm, to add more length to body without rep chart, work sc rounds using C until desired length, making sure to turn at end of every round and finish on a WS round.

Fasten off.

On RS count 4 (5, 5, 5, 5) (6, 6, 7, 7) sts to left of fasten off point and join C to next st leaving those 4 (5, 5, 5, 5) (6, 6, 7, 7) sts empty.

Row 1: 1 ch, skip first st, 55 (59, 65, 77, 83) (87, 99, 103, 109) sc, sc2tog, turn. 56 (60, 66, 78, 84) (88, 100, 104, 110) sts

Underarm dec row: 1 ch, skip first st, sc to last 2 sts, sc2tog, turn. 54 (58, 64, 76, 82) (86, 98, 102, 108) sts – 2 sts dec

Rep Underarm Dec Row 3 (4, 4, 8, 10) (11, 17, 18, 21) more times. 48 (50, 56, 60, 62) (64, 64, 66, 66) sts

Work 4 (3, 5, 2, 2) (3, 0, 0, 0) more rows of sc without dec before cont with neck.

FRONT NECK 1ST SIDE

Row 1: 1 ch, 16 (17, 19, 21, 21) (22, 22, 23, 23) sc, sc2tog, turn. 17 (18, 20, 22, 22) (23, 23, 24, 24) sts

Row 2: 1 ch, skip first st, sc to end of row, turn. 16 (17, 19, 21, 21) (22, 22, 23, 23) sts – 1 st dec

Row 3: 1 ch, sc to last 2 sts, sc2tog, turn. 15 (16, 18, 20, 20) (21, 21, 22, 22) sts – 1 st dec

Rep prev two rows 2 (3, 4, 4, 4) (4, 4, 4, 4) more times. 11 (10, 10, 12, 12) (13, 13, 14, 14) sts

SIZES 1 (4) (6, 7, 8, 9) ONLY

Rep Row 2 once more. 10 (11) (12, 12, 13, 13) sts

Chart 1

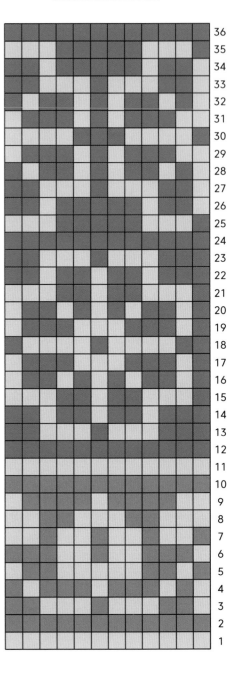

KEY

A ☐ B ◼ C ◼

Work from the bottom up and right to left. Each square represents one scBLO st.

Remember to 1 ch at beg of every round and use invisible join throughout (see General Techniques: Invisible Join When Working in Rounds), always working on RS.

STRAP

Work sc rows until strap measures approx 8¾ (9¼, 9⅞, 10⅜, 10¾) (11½, 11¾, 12⅜, 12¾) in/22.5 (23.5, 25, 26.5, 27.5) (29, 30, 31.5, 32.5) cm from bottom of underarm or until desired length (remember fabric will stretch much easier at this point than at body).

Fasten off.

FRONT NECK 2ND SIDE

Start on same RS or WS as First Side.

Count 12 (12, 14, 14, 16) (16, 16, 16, 16) sts from last worked st at Front Neck. Leave those sts empty and join C to next st.

Row 1: 1 ch, skip first st (where yarn was joined), sc to end of row, turn. 17 (18, 20, 22, 22) (23, 23, 24, 24) sts – 1 st dec

Row 2: 1 ch, sc to last 2 sts, sc2tog, turn. 16 (17, 19, 21, 21) (22, 22, 23, 23) sts – 1 st dec

Rep prev two rows 3 (3, 4, 5, 4) (5, 5, 5, 5) more times. 10 (11, 11, 11, 13) (12, 12, 13, 13) sts

SIZES 2 (3, 5) ONLY
Rep Row 1 once more. 10 (10,12) sts

ALL SIZES
Rep Strap on this side.

BACK

On RS, count 8 (10, 10, 10, 10) (12, 12, 14, 14) sts from where Front ends and leave empty for underarm, join C to next st.

SIZES 1 AND 2 ONLY
Skip to Back Neck First Side.

SIZES 3 (4, 5) (6, 7, 8, 9) ONLY
Row 1: 1 ch, skip st where yarn was attached, 65 (77, 83) (87, 99, 103, 109) sc, sc2tog, turn. 66 (78, 84) (88, 100, 104, 110) sts

Underarm dec row: 1 ch, skip first st, sc to last 2 sts, sc2tog, turn. 64 (76, 82) (86, 98, 102, 108) sts – 2 sts dec

Rep Underarm Dec Row 0 (1, 3) (5, 5, 8, 10) more times. 64, (74, 76) (76, 88, 86, 86) sts

**BACK NECK 1ST SIDE

Row 1: 1 ch, skip first st, 20 (22, 22, 27, 27) (27, 33, 32, 33) sc, sc2tog, turn. 21 (23, 23, 28, 28) (28, 34, 33, 34) sts

Neck and underarm shaping row: 1 ch, skip first st, sc to last 2 sts of row, sc2tog, turn. 19 (21, 21, 26, 26) (26, 32, 31, 32) sts – 2 sts dec

Rep Neck and Underarm Shaping Row 3 (4, 2, 5, 5) (4, 10, 8, 9) more times. 13 (13, 17, 16, 16) (18, 12, 15, 14) sts

SIZES 1 (2, 3, 4, 5) (6, 8, 9) ONLY
Stop dec at underarm side and dec 1 at neck side for next 3 (3, 7, 5, 4) (6, 2, 1) rows by skipping first st on rows that start at neckline or sc2tog on rows that start at underarm end. 10 (10, 10, 11, 12) (12, 12, 13, 13) sts

STRAP

Work sc rows until strap measures approx 8¾ (9¼, 9⅞, 10⅜, 10¾) (11½, 11¾, 12⅜, 12¾) in/22.5 (23.5, 25, 26.5, 27.5) (29, 30, 31.5, 32.5) cm from bottom of underarm or until desired length.

Fasten off.**

BACK NECK AND UNDERARM SHAPING 2ND SIDE

Start on same RS or WS as Back Neck First Side.

Count 12 (12, 14, 14, 16) (16, 16, 16, 16) sts from last worked st at Front Neck. Leave those sts empty and join C to next st.

Rep from ** to **.

Join Straps tog at shoulder by sewing last rows of each together on WS. Make sure to join Front straps to Back Straps and avoid any twisting.

NECKLINE EDGING

Note: When working in row ends, adjust number of sts made so edging is not too loose.

Join C to a shoulder seam on RS.

Round 1: 1 ch, sc around neckline, making sc2tog in corners where middle of neck at Front and Back meets neck shaping, slst to join round and change to A.

Fasten off C.

Round 2: 1 ch, scBLO around, slst to join round.

Fasten off A.

ARMHOLE EDGING

Join C to middle of underarm on WS.

Round 1: 1 ch, sc around armhole opening, making sc2tog in corners where middle of underarm meets underarm shaping rows, slst to join round and change to A.

Fasten off C.

Round 2: 1 ch, scBLO around, slst to join round.

Fasten off A.

Rep around other armhole.

Finishing

Weave in all ends and block to measurements.

Ailyak pullover

Ailyak (Bulgarian) — the art of doing everything slowly with no rush, while enjoying the process and life in general; like the Swahili 'hakuna matata'.

See Project Information for finished size dimensions.

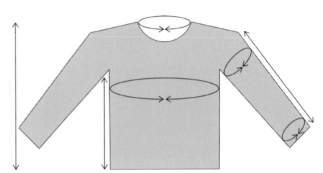

SIZES
9 sizes (1–9)

YARN
Less Traveled Yarn Tweed Me Sock (85% merino wool, 15% Donegal nep), fingering (2ply), 100g (438yd/400m), in the following color:
A: Jack Pine; 3¼ (3½, 4, 4¼, 4¾) (5¼, 5½, 6, 6½) skeins
Less Traveled Yarn Coupe (80% merino wool, 10% cashmere, 10% nylon) sport (3ply), 100g (382yd/349m), in the following color:
B: Vice; 2¼ (2½, 2¾, 3, 3¼) (3½, 3¾, 4, 4½) skeins

TOOLS
US size D (3mm) hook
US size E/4 (3.5mm) hook
5 stitch markers

GAUGE (TENSION)
24 sts x 19 rows measure 4 x 4in (10 x 10cm) over extended single crochet colorwork in the round using a US size D (3mm) hook.

SPECIAL ABBREVIATION
esc, extended single crochet: insert hook in st, yo, pull through st, yo, pull through one loop on hook, yo, pull through rem loops on hook

This pullover represents the beauty of slowing down and enjoying life in general, a reminder to see the flowers grow and stop to smell them. Its top-down construction makes it very adjustable and seamless, while providing a comfortable fit around neck and shoulders. The tapestry colorwork in the yoke, body and sleeves will keep you interested during the process of making the jumper and the result is a striking piece of clothing that will elevate any wardrobe.

NOTES

The pullover is worked top-down, starting at the slip stitch ribbed neckline—keep stitches loose so you can work into them and to keep the elasticity of the ribbing. Short rows are worked at the back of the neck for a better fit around neck and shoulders. The yoke is worked in circles using the chart and written instructions, while at the same time increasing throughout. Once the yoke is complete the body is separated from the sleeves and worked to the desired length, then finished with a ribbed hem. The sleeves are then worked and finished with a ribbed cuff.

Other than the short rows, ribbed neck, cuffs and bottom hem, the entire garment is worked in extended single crochet. There are color charts to follow for the yoke, body and sleeves (see Colorwork Techniques: Tapestry Crochet).

Use an invisible join (see General Techniques: Invisible Join When Working in Rounds) to join rounds throughout.

Main body

NECKLINE

Using US size E/4 hook and A, ch 11 (or as many chains as desired width of ribbing).

Row 1: Skip first ch, slst in each ch, turn. 10 sts

Row 2: 1 ch, slstBLO to end of row, turn. 10 sts

Rep Row 2 for a total of 130 (132, 132, 136, 144) (144, 144, 144, 148) rows or until ribbing measures approx 19 (19¼, 19¼, 19⅞, 21¼) (21¼, 21¼, 21¼, 21¾) in/48 (49, 49, 50.5, 54) (54, 54, 54, 55.5) cm, WITHOUT much stretching making sure it fits over your head.

On WS, slst tog FLO of last worked row and starting chain. Turn work inside out to work on side edge of ribbing on RS.

Set-up round: Using US size D hook, sc around on side of ribbing making sure you have a total of 130 (132, 132, 136, 144) (144, 144, 144, 148) sts, slst in first st to join round.

Note: You may need to work one st every 2 rows of ribbing in places if you made more than the recommended number of rows.

SHORT ROWS

Row 1 will go to one side, inc twice, turn; Row 2 will return to center of back without inc, then cont onto other side, inc twice, and turn. Row 3 will return to center of back again and close round. Use invisible join to join short row rounds; the join will run at center back.

There are 2 (3, 3, 3, 3) (3, 3, 3, 3) sets in total.

Row 1 (RS): 1 ch (doesn't count as a st throughout), 1 sc in first st, PM to mark beg of round, 12 (11, 11, 12, 13) (13, 13, 13, 12) sc, 2 sc in next st, PM in first st of inc, 26 (24, 24, 24, 27) (27, 27, 27, 29) sc, 2 sc in next st, PM in second st of inc, 4 (4, 4, 4, 3) (3, 3, 3, 4) sc, turn. 47 (44, 44, 45, 48) (48, 48, 48, 50) sts

Row 2 (WS): 1 ch, skip first st, sc to beg of round moving all markers up, sc in beg of round and PM, 1 ch (doesn't count as a st), 12 (11, 11, 12, 13) (13, 13, 13, 12) sc, 2 sc in next st, PM in first st of inc, 26 (24, 24, 24, 27) (27, 27, 27, 29) sc, 2 sc in next st, PM in second st of inc, 4 (4, 4, 4, 3) (3, 3, 3, 4) sc, turn. 92 (86, 86, 88, 94) (94, 94, 94, 98) sts

Row 3 (RS): 1 ch, skip first st, sc to beg of round moving all markers up, slst in beg of round to join round. 45 (42, 42, 43, 46) (46, 46, 46, 48) sts

First set of short rows completed.

Row 4 (RS): 1 ch, sc in first st (beg of round) and PM, *sc to before marker, 2 sc in marked st* and PM in first st of inc; rep from * to * and PM in second st of inc, sc to "step" left at end of prev short row, sc in "step", sc in next 4 sts of neck, turn. 53 (50, 50, 51, 54) (54, 54, 54, 56) sts

Row 5 (WS): 1 ch, skip first st, sc to beg of round moving all markers up, sc in beg of round and PM, 1 ch (doesn't count as a st), *sc to before marker, 2 sc in marked st* and PM in first st of inc; rep from * to * and PM in second st of inc, sc to "step" left at end of prev short row, sc in "step", sc in next 4 sts of neck, turn. 104 (98, 98, 100, 106) (106, 106, 106, 110) sts

Row 6 (RS): 1 ch, skip first st, sc to beg of round moving all markers up, slst in beg of round to join round. 51 (48, 48, 49, 52) (52, 52, 52, 54) sts

Second set of short rows completed.

SIZE 1 ONLY

Skip ahead to Yoke.

SIZES 2 TO 9 ONLY

Rep Rows 4 to 6 once more.

At this point, there are 51 (54, 54, 55, 58) (58, 58, 58, 60) sts each side of beg of round st; a total of 138 (144, 144, 148, 156) (156, 156, 156, 160) sts around neck incl: 103 (109, 109, 111, 117) (117, 117, 117, 121) sts at Back, 2 short row steps, and 33 (33, 33, 35, 37) (37, 37, 37, 37) unworked neck sts at Front.

YOKE

Remove markers. Start working in esc rounds on RS only. Work Inc Round 1 and then foll colorwork chart inc where indicated. Inc Round 1 is first to go around whole neck. Work increases (inc1) when indicated. Work on "steps" formed by short rows as on a normal st.

SIZES 1 (3, 4) (8, 9) ONLY

Inc round 1: 1 ch, 6 (0, 4) (0, 0) esc, [inc1, 10 (17, 11) (12, 7) esc] 12 (8, 12) (12, 20) times around, slst in first st to join round. 150 (152, 160) (168, 180) sts

SIZES 2 (7) ONLY

Inc round 1: 1 ch, 1 (2) esc, [4 (2) esc, inc1, 5 (3) esc, inc1] 13 (22) times, slst in first st to join round. 170 (200) sts

SIZE 5 ONLY

Inc round 1: 1 ch, inc1, 3 esc, [inc1, 7 esc] 19 times around, slst in first st to join round. 176 sts

SIZE 6 ONLY

Inc round 1: 1 ch, [inc1, 3 esc, inc1, 3 esc, inc1, 4 esc] 12 times around, slst in first st to join round. 192 sts

ALL SIZES

Work Yoke charts 1 and 2.

SIZES 1 TO 7 ONLY

Move on to Body and Sleeves Separation Round after finishing row 37 (38, 39, 40, 41) (44, 46) of Chart 2.

SIZES 8 AND 9 ONLY

After finishing Chart 2, work 2 more rows of plain esc using A before continuing with Body and Sleeves Separation Round.

ALL SIZES

Note: Before working Separation Round, try on yoke and adjust length to desired measurements for a perfect fit. You may add more or remove rounds, making sure to cont foll chart if Chart 2 hasn't been completed, or working plain rounds in esc using A.

Body and sleeves separation round:
1 ch, 45 (50, 54, 59, 66) (72, 75, 83, 90) esc (Back), 5 (5, 7, 7, 9) (7, 11, 9, 11) ch for first underarm, skip 60 (70, 82, 82, 89) (97, 101, 114, 121) sts (First Sleeve), 91 (101, 109, 119, 131) (143, 149, 167, 179) esc (Front), 5 (5, 7, 7, 9) (7, 11, 9, 11) ch for second underarm, skip 60 (70, 82, 82, 89) (97, 101, 114, 121) sts (Second Sleeve), esc to end of round, slst in first st to join round. 190 (210, 230, 250, 280) (300, 320, 350, 380) sts incl underarm ch

Note: If Chart 2 wasn't completed before Separation Round, make sure to foll it when working Back and Front sts and to make underarm chains using A. Carry B at underarm to cont using it afterwards.

For foll rounds, until Chart 2 is completed, work around Body EXCEPT at underarms working esc using A and carrying B along instead.

Yoke chart 1

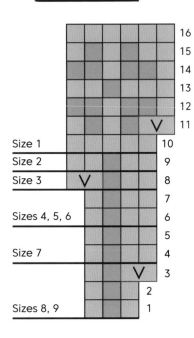

Size 1 — 10
Size 2 — 9
Size 3 — 8
— 7
Sizes 4, 5, 6 — 6
— 5
Size 7 — 4
— 3
— 2
Sizes 8, 9 — 1

Rows (from top): 16, 15, 14, 13, 12, 11

KEY

| A | B | V 2 esc in same st (inc1) |

Read chart from bottom up and right to left. Each box represents one stitch worked in extended single crochet (esc).

Rep each row a total of 30 (34, 38, 40, 44) (48, 50, 56, 60) times around, omitting rows that don't correspond to chosen size.

Work 1 ch at beg of every round and use invisible join throughout.

Stitch count totals:

Rows 1 and 3: – (–, –, –, –) (–, –, 168, 180)
Rows 4 to 7: – (–, –, 160, 176) (192, 200, 224, 240)
Rows 8 to 10: 150 (170, 190, 200, 220) (240, 250, 280, 300)
Rows 11 to 16: 180 (204, 228, 240, 264) (288, 300, 336, 360)
Rows 17 and 18: 210 (238, 266, 280, 308) (336, 350, 392, 420)
Rows 19 to 22: 240 (272, 304, 320, 352) (384, 400, 448, 480)
Rows 21 to 22: 270 (306, 342, 360, 396) (432, 450, 504, 540)
Row 23: 255 (289, 323, 340, 374) (408, 425, 476, 510)
Rows 24 to 27: 270 (306, 342, 360, 396) (432, 450, 504, 540)
Row 28 onward: 300 (340, 380, 400, 440) (480, 500, 560, 600)

Yoke chart 2 (sizes 1 to 5)

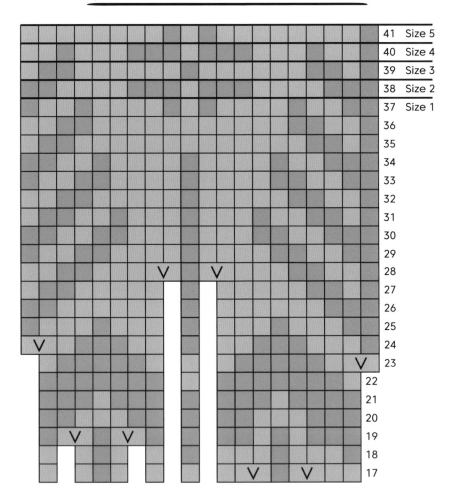

41 Size 5
40 Size 4
39 Size 3
38 Size 2
37 Size 1
36
35
34
33
32
31
30
29
28
27
26
25
24
23
22
21
20
19
18
17

Yoke chart 2 (sizes 6 to 9)

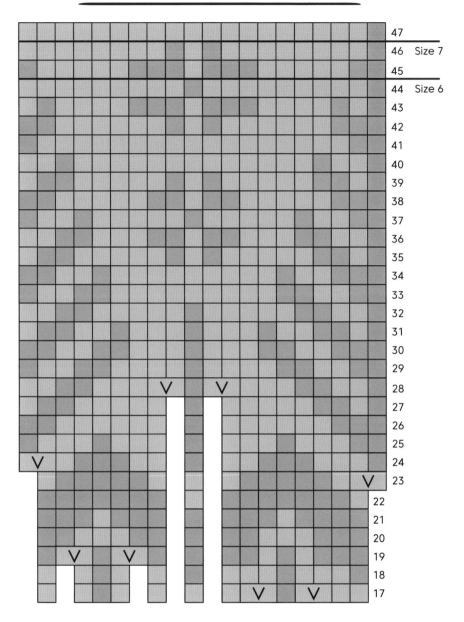

47	
46	Size 7
45	
44	Size 6
43	
42	
41	
40	
39	
38	
37	
36	
35	
34	
33	
32	
31	
30	
29	
28	
27	
26	
25	
24	
23	
22	
21	
20	
19	
18	
17	

KEY

☐ A ▦ B **V** 2 esc in same st (inc1)

Read chart from bottom up and right to left. Each box represents one stitch worked in extended single crochet (esc).

Sizes 1-5: Rep each row a total of 15 (17, 19, 20, 22) times around.

Sizes 6-9: Rep each row a total of (24, 25, 28, 30) times around.

Body chart 1

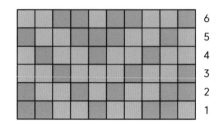

6
5
4
3
2
1

Body chart 2

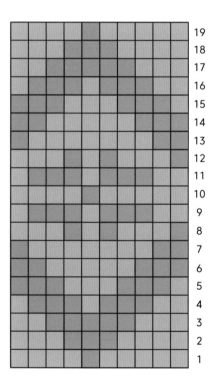

19
18
17
16
15
14
13
12
11
10
9
8
7
6
5
4
3
2
1

BODY

Stitch count will remain constant throughout. Work around body making sure to work 1 ch at beg of every round and use invisible join throughout.

Finish Yoke chart 2 on Front and Back sts (not at underarm) if it hasn't been done already.

Using A, work 3 rows of plain esc (if you worked plain rows in yoke or separation round, count them towards these three).

Work Body chart 1, then work 3 rows of plain esc using A.

Work Body chart 2, then work 3 rows of plain esc using A.

For a cropped sweater, skip ahead to Bottom Ribbing. For a full length sweater, repeat Body charts 1 and 2 once more making 3 rows of plain esc using A between them and finishing with 3 more plain rows.

Feel free to adjust length by rep charts as many times as desired and stopping at desired length from underarm minus 1½in (4cm) of ribbing.

BOTTOM RIBBING

Using US size E/4 hook and A, ch 13.

Row 1: Starting in second ch from hook, slst to end of ch, when reaching body, skip very first st of round and slst in next st. 12 sts of ribbing

Row 2: Slst in next st, turn, skip 2 slsts done on body, slstBLO to end of row, turn. 12 sts

Row 3: 1 ch, slstBLO to end of row, slst in next empty st of body. 12 sts

Rep Rows 2 and 3 around bottom edge of body. On WS, join FLO of each st of last row of ribbing to each starting ch of ribbing with slsts.

Fasten off.

KEY

 A   B

Read charts from bottom up and right to left. Each box represents one stitch worked in extended single crochet (esc).

Rep each row a total of 19 (21, 23, 25, 28) (30, 32, 35, 38) times around.

Sleeves

(work one in each sleeve opening)

Using US size D hook, join A to middle of underarm to work on RS on unused loops of starting ch.

Set-up round: esc to end of underarm, esc around yoke sleeve sts, esc to end of round, slst in first st to join round. Approx 65 (75, 89, 89, 98) (104, 112, 123, 132) sts

Notes: work esc2tog in corners where underarm meets yoke to close any gaps if necessary.

If Yoke chart 2 wasn't finished before Separation Round, foll chart on Sleeve Yoke sts (not underarm sts) starting where necessary to match what was done before. Work until Yoke chart 2 is complete.

Read ahead to learn Color and Shaping patts.

COLOR PATT

Finish Yoke chart 2 (not at underarm) if it hasn't been done already.

Work 3 rows of plain esc using A; if you have already worked plain rows in yoke, count them towards these three.

Work Body chart 1, then work 3 rows of plain esc using A.

Work Body chart 2, then work 3 rows of plain esc using A.

The previous paragraph sets color patt.

Note: Last rep of chart might not fit entirely if sleeve stitch count cannot be divided by 10. This disparity will be on underside of arm, so won't be visible.

SHAPING PATT

Cont to work color patt while AT THE SAME TIME, shape sleeve as foll:

Work in color patt for 2⅜in (6cm), then work a Dec Round.

Dec round: 1 ch, esc2tog, esc around to last 2 sts, esc2tog, slst in first st to join round. Make sure to foll color patt as corresponds to match prev round. 2 sts dec

Work 7 (4, 2, 2, 2) (1, 1, 1, 1) rounds of color patt.

Rep Dec Round.

Cont shaping sleeves working color patt and a Dec Round every eighth (5th, 3rd, 3rd, 3rd) (2nd, 2nd, 2nd, 2nd) round until desired sleeve circumference, or until there are approx 3 (6, 9, 9, 10) (11, 13, 15, 17) Dec Rounds worked for a three-quarter length sleeve and 7 (12, 18, 18, 21) (23, 26, 31, 35) Dec Rounds worked for a full-length sleeve.

Notes: As you rep chart around and dec 1 st at beg and of round on Dec Rounds, starting point of chart will shift: after first Dec Round, chart will start on stitch two, and so on.

Work color patt until desired sleeve length minus 1½in (4cm) of ribbing; or approx 9⅞in (25 cm) for three-quarter length sleeve or 14¾ (15⅛, 15⅛, 15¾, 15¾) (16⅛, 16⅛, 16¾, 16¾) in/37.5 (38.5, 38.5, 40, 40) (41, 41, 42.5, 42.5) cm for full length sleeve.

CUFF

Rep ribbing as for bottom of body.

Finishing

Weave in all ends and block to measurements.

Hygge jacket

Hygge (Danish) — a quality of coziness and comfortable conviviality that engenders a feeling of contentment or well-being (regarded as a defining characteristic of Danish culture).

See Project Information for finished size dimensions.

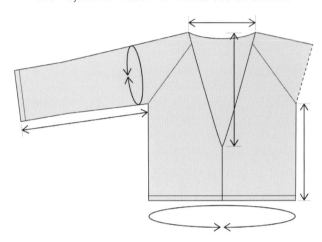

SIZES

9 sizes (1–9)

YARN

Knit Picks Wool of Andes Tweed (80% Peruvian wool, 20% Donegal Tweed), worsted (aran), 50g (109½yd/100m) in the following colors:

A: Down Hear; 6¾ (7½, 8½, 9¾, 11½) (13, 14¼, 16, 17¾) skeins

B: Flagstone Hear; 2½ (2¾, 3, 3, 3½) (3¾, 4, 4¼, 4½) skeins

Knit Picks Wool of Andes (100% Peruvian wool), worsted (aran), 50g (109½yd/100m) in following color:

C: Sapphire Hear; 2 (2¼, 2¼, 2½, 2¾) (3, 3½, 3½, 3½) skeins

TOOLS

US size H/8 (5mm) hook
4 stitch markers

GAUGE (TENSION)

15 sts x 18 rows measure 4 x 4in (10 x 10cm) over single crochet using a US size H/8 (5mm) hook.

SPECIAL ABBREVIATIONS

mdc, mosaic double crochet: dc in skipped st of same color 3 rows below, working in front of intervening 2 rows of ch in other color

rsc, reverse single crochet (crab st): 1 ch, *insert hook in next st to right, yo, pull through st keeping new loop on hook to left of loop already on hook (closer to tip of hook not handle), yo working yarn, pull through two loops on hook; rep from * to last st of row, slst in last st of row

This jacket embodies coziness and comfort; it's what you would wear on a cool summer evening with friends, or while cuddling your family on a chilly morning. Its simple raglan construction in worsted weight (aran) yarn means fast progress to keep you entertained, while the border at the bottom of the body and sleeves is the perfect introduction to mosaic crochet. The sample shown has a cropped length and three-quarter sleeves, but the jacket would be just as effective as a tunic length. The reverse single crochet makes a beautiful rope-like edging.

NOTES

The jacket is worked top-down with raglan shoulder shaping. The yoke is divided into five sections: two fronts, a back and two sleeves. Increases are worked at four raglan corners between sections and at the front to shape neckline. Once the yoke is complete, the body is separated from the sleeves, with a mosaic crochet motif added to the bottom (see Colorwork Techniques: Mosaic Crochet, Standard Mosaic Crochet), and finished with a reverse single crochet edging. The wide sleeves are worked in rounds without shaping in openings left on the yoke, turning at the end of every round for stitch consistency, and finishing with the same mosaic pattern. The jacket is finished with a ribbed neckline.

Yoke

Using A, ch 44 (40, 36, 40, 44) (50, 54, 60, 54).

Row 1: 3 sc in second ch, PM in middle st of inc (raglan marker 1), 11 (6, 4, 4, 4) (6, 8, 9, 4) sc, 3 sc in next ch, PM in middle st of inc (raglan marker 2), 17 (23, 23, 27, 31) (33, 33, 37, 41) sc, 3 sc in next ch, PM in middle st of inc (raglan marker 3), 11 (6, 4, 4, 4) (6, 8, 9, 4) sc, 3 sc in next ch, PM in middle st of inc (raglan marker 4), turn. 51 (47, 43, 47, 51) (57, 61, 67, 61) sts = 1 st at each Front, 19 (25, 25, 29, 33) (35, 35, 39, 43) at Back, 13 (8, 6, 6, 6) (8, 10, 11, 6) at each sleeve, 4 Raglan sts

From now on, there will be four kinds of rows on yoke. Foll table provided and work corresponding instructions on each row.

Raglan only inc row (R): 1 ch (doesn't count as st throughout), *sc to before marker, inc2 in marked st, PM in middle st of inc; rep from * 3 more times, sc to end of row, turn. 8 sts inc

Raglan and neck inc row (R+N): 1 ch (doesn't count as st throughout), inc1 in first st, *sc to before marker, inc2 in marked st, PM in middle st of inc; rep from * 3 more times, sc to last st, inc1 in last st of row, turn. 10 sts inc

Neck only inc row (N): 1 ch, inc1 in first st, sc to last st moving all markers up, inc1 in last st of row, turn. 2 sts inc

No inc rows (N/I): 1 ch, sc in each st of row moving all markers up, turn.

YOKE PROGRESS TABLE

Foll corresponding size and use written instructions provided for each kind of row. Numbers to right of each row represent st count. Row 1 of table corresponds to Row 1 of written instructions.

	SIZE 1	SIZE 2	SIZE 3	SIZE 4	SIZE 5	SIZE 6	SIZE 7	SIZE 8	SIZE 9
Row 1	R 51	R 47	R 43	R 47	R 51	R 57	R 61	R 67	R 61
Row 2	R 59	R 55	R 51	R 55	R+N 61	R+N 67	R 69	R 75	R 69
Row 3	R 67	R 63	R+N 61	R 63	R 69	R 75	R 77	R 83	R 77
Row 4	N/I 67	N/I 63	N/I 61	R+N 73	N/I 69	N/I 75	N/I 77	N 85	N 79
Row 5	R+N 77	R+N 73	R 69	R 81	R 77	R 83	R+N 87	R 93	R 87
Row 6	R 85	R 81	R+N 79	N/I 81	R+N 87	R+N 93	R 95	R 101	R 95
Row 7	R 93	R 89	R 87	R 89	R 95	R 101	R 103	R+N 111	R+N 105
Row 8	N/I 93	N/I 89	N/I 87	R+N 99	N/I 95	N/I 101	N 105	N/I 111	N/I 105
Row 9	R 101	R 97	R+N 97	R 107	R 103	R 109	R 113	R 119	R 113
Row 10	R 109	R+N 107	R 105	N/I 107	R+N 113	R+N 119	R 121	R+N 129	R+N 123
Row 11	R 117	R 115	R 113	R 115	R 121	R 127	R 129	R 137	R 131
Row 12	N 119	N/I 115	N 115	R+N 125	N/I 121	N/I 127	N 131	N/I 137	N/I 131
Row 13	R 127	R 123	R 123	R 133	R 129	R 135	R 139	R+N 147	R+N 141
Row 14	N/I 127	R 131	N/I 123	N/I 133	R+N 139	R+N 145	R 147	R 155	R 149
Row 15	R 135	R+N 141	R+N 133	R 141	R 147	R 153	R+N 157	R 163	R 157
Row 16	N/I 135	N/I 141	N/I 133	N 143	N/I 147	N/I 153	N/I 157	N 165	N 159
Row 17	R 143	R 149	R 141	R 151	R 155	R 161	R 165	R 173	R 167
Row 18	N/I 143	N/I 149	N 143	N/I 151	R+N 165	R+N 171	R+N 175	R 181	R 175
Row 19	R 151	R 157	R 151	R 159	R 173	R 179	R 183	R+N 191	R+N 185
Row 20	R+N 161	N 159	N/I 151	N 161	N/I 173	N/I 179	N/I 183	N/I 191	N/I 185

	SIZE 1	SIZE 2	SIZE 3	SIZE 4	SIZE 5	SIZE 6	SIZE 7	SIZE 8	SIZE 9
Row 21	R 169	R 167	R+N 161	R 169	R 181	R 187	R+N 193	R 199	R 193
Row 22	N/I 169	N/I 167	N/I 161	N/I 169	R+N 191	R+N 197	R 201	R+N 209	R+N 203
Row 23	R 177	R 175	R 169	R 177	R 199	R 205	R 209	R 217	R 211
Row 24	N/I 177	N/I 175	N 171	N 179	N/I 199	N/I 205	N 211	N/I 217	N/I 211
Row 25	R 185	R+N 185	R 179	R 187	R 207	R 213	R 219	R+N 227	R+N 221
Row 26	N 187	N/I 185	N/I 179	N/I 187	N 209	N 215	R 227	R 235	R 229
Row 27	R 195	R 193	R+N 189	R 195	R 217	R 223	R+N 237	R 243	R 237
Row 28	N/I 195	N/I 193	N/I 189	N 197	N/I 217	N/I 223	N/I 237	N 245	N 239
Row 29	R 203	R 201	R 197	R 205	R 225	R 231	R 245	R 253	R 247
Row 30	N/I 203	N 203	N 199	N/I 205	N 227	N 233	N 247	R 261	R 255
Row 31	R 211	R 211	R 207	R 213	R 235	R 241	R 255	R+N 271	R+N 265
Row 32	N 213	N/I 211	N/I 207	N 215	N/I 235	N/I 241	N/I 255	N/I 271	N/I 265
Row 33	N/I 213	R 219	R+N 217	R 223	R 243	R 249	R+N 265	R 279	R 273
Row 34		N/I 219	N/I 217	N/I 223	N 245	N 251	N/I 265	N 281	N 275
Row 35		R+N 229	R 225	R 231	R 253	R 259	R 273	R 289	R 283
Row 36		N/I 229	N/I 225	N 233	N/I 253	N/I 259	N 275	N/I 289	N/I 283
Row 37			R 233	R 241	R 261	R 267	R 283	R+N 299	R+N 293
Row 38			N/I 233	N/I 241	N 263	N 269	N/I 283	N/I 299	N/I 293
Row 39			R 241	R 249	R 271	R 277	R+N 293	R 307	R 301
Row 40			N/I 241	N 251	N/I 271	N/I 277	N/I 293	N 309	N 303
Row 41				R 259	R+N 281	R 285	R 301	R 317	R 311
Row 42				R 267	N/I 281	N 287	N 303	N/I 317	N/I 311
Row 43				N/I 267	R 289	R 295	R 311	R+N 327	R+N 321
Row 44					N 291	N/I 295	N/I 311	N/I 327	N/I 321
Row 45					R 299	R 303	R+N 321	R 335	R 329
Row 46					N/I 299	N 305	N/I 321	N/I 335	N 331
Row 47						R 313	R 329	R 343	R 339
Row 48						N/I 313	N/I 329	N/I 343	N/I 339
Row 49						R 321	R 337	R 351	R+N 349
Row 50						N/I 321	N/I 337	N/I 351	N/I 349
Row 51							R 345	R 359	R 357
Row 52							N/I 345	N/I 359	N 359
Row 53							N/I 345	R 367	R 367
Row 54								N/I 367	N/I 367
Row 55								N/I 367	R 375
Row 56									N/I 375
Row 57									R 383
Row 58									N/I 383
Row 59									N/I 383

Chart 1

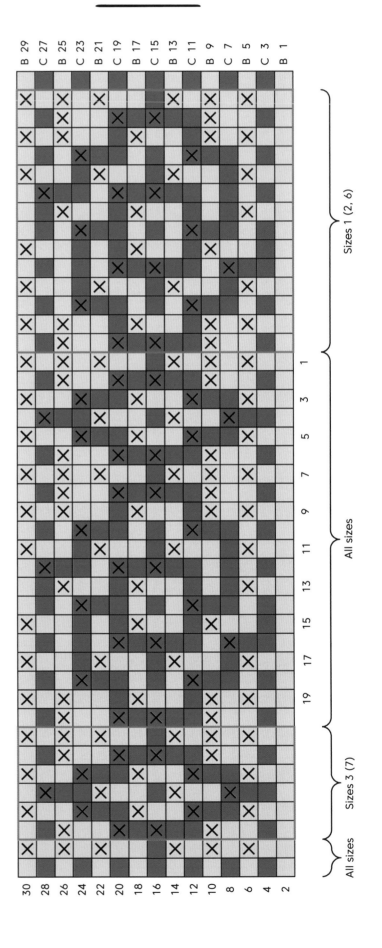

Chart 2

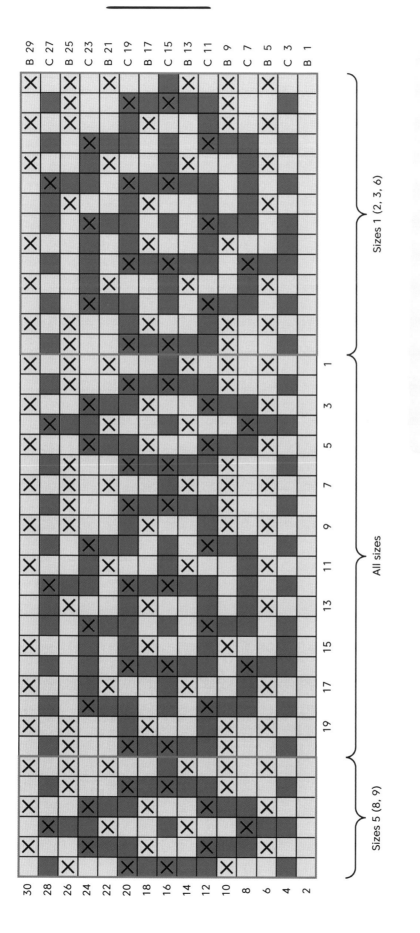

KEY

- ☐ B
- ■ C

X mosaic double crochet (mdc)

To work from these charts, rotate 90 degrees clockwise.

Read the chart from bottom up, from right to left on RS rows, and left to right on WS rows. Each square represents 1 stitch and each chart row represents 2 rows of crochet.

Make 1 ch at start of each row.

Chart 2: Join round with invisible join and turn at end of each round.

Charts follow all Standard Mosaic Crochet rules (see Colorwork Techniques: Mosaic Crochet).

BODY

There is now a total of 213 (229, 241, 267, 299) (321, 345, 367, 383) sts on yoke; 26 (30, 35, 37, 42) (44, 48, 50, 55) sts at each front, incl marked raglan stitches 1 and 4; 51 (50, 50, 56, 62) (68, 74, 79, 78) sts for each sleeve between markers; and 59 (69, 71, 81, 91) (97, 101, 109, 117) sts at back, incl marked raglan stitches 2 and 3.

Note: Before working Separation Row, try on yoke and adjust length to desired depth for a perfect fit. Add more or remove No Inc Rows as desired.

Body and sleeves separation row:
1 ch, sc to and incl marked st, 3 (4, 4, 4, 4) (6, 6, 7, 8) ch for underarm, skip sleeve sts between markers, sc from next marker to foll marker for Back incl marked sts, 3 (4, 4, 4, 4) (6, 6, 7, 8) ch for underarm, skip sleeve sts between markers, sc from marked st to end of row, turn. 117 (137, 149, 163, 183) (197, 209, 223 243) sts incl underarm ch

Remove all markers.

Next row: 1 ch, sc around body incl at underarm, turn. 117 (137, 149, 163, 183) (197, 209, 223 243) sts

Work 2 more sc rows around body or until desired length minus 7in (18cm)

of bottom motif and edging. Until now, RS and WS look identical; last worked row will determine WS so that next row is on RS.

Change to B on last st of prev row and work Chart 1 along bottom of body.

Fasten off A.

SIZES 1 (2, 6) ONLY
Rep 20 st chart 5 (6, 9) times. Omit second red box.

SIZES 3 (7) ONLY
Omit first red box, rep 20 st chart 7 (10) times.

SIZES 4 (5, 8, 9) ONLY
Omit both red boxes, rep 20 st chart 8 (9, 11, 12) times.

ALL SIZES
Once chart is complete, change to A and fasten off B and C.

EDGING

Row 1 (RS): 1 ch, sc to end of row.

Fasten off.

Sleeves

(make one in each opening)

Join A to middle of underarm.

If last row of Yoke was RS row, make next row on WS and vice versa.

Set-up round: Sc to end of underarm, around yoke sleeve sts, and to end of round, slst in first st to join round, turn. 54 (54, 54, 60, 66) (74, 80, 86, 86) sts

Notes: Work sc2tog in corners where underarm meets yoke to close any gaps if necessary—make sure your st count is correct.

From now on, turn at end of every round. Use invisible join throughout (see General Techniques: Invisible join).

Work sc rounds for next 6¼in (16cm), or until desired sleeve length minus 7in (18cm) of bottom motif and edging, making sure to finish on WS row to start chart on RS on foll row.

Fasten off A, change to B on last st of previous row and work Chart 2 around sleeve.

SIZES 1 (2, 3, 6) ONLY
Rep 20 st chart 2 (2, 2, 3) times, omit second red box.

SIZES 4 (7) ONLY
Omit both red boxes, rep 20 st chart 3 (4) times.

SIZES 5 (8, 9) ONLY
Omit first red box, rep 20 st chart 3 (4, 4) times.

ALL SIZES
Once Chart 2 is complete, change to A and fasten off B and C.

EDGING

Row 1 (RS): 1 ch, sc to end of round, slst in first st to join round, do not turn.

Row 2: 1ch, rsc to end of round.

Fasten off, leaving a tail to weave in later.

NECKLINE EDGING

Find raglan inc that flank Back on starting ch (where raglan markers 2 and 3 were located on Row 1), PM on both ch. Join A to bottom right corner of Front on RS to work along vertical edge of Front, 1 ch, sc along front at approx 3 sts every 4 rows until before first back marker, sc2tog over marked st and next st, sc along back of neckline until 1 st before next Back marker, sc2tog , sc to bottom corner at Front. Remove all markers.

Note: Total number of sts in this row is not important, as long as fabric is not too tight so that ribbing doesn't shrink band later on, nor too loose so that Front is longer than rest of jacket.

Now PM where starting ch of yoke started and ended (where raglan markers 1 and 4 were located on Row 1) and also approx where neckline shaping ends at both sides of Front (lowest point of V-neck). Check there are same number of sts between markers at each side of front.

NECKLINE RIBBING

Cont where you left off after edging at bottom left corner of Front, 11 ch.

Row 1: Starting in second ch from hook, sc to end of ch, when reaching body, skip first st of row and slst in next st. 10 sts of ribbing

Row 2: Slst in next st, turn, skip 2 slsts done on body, scBLO to end of row, turn. 10 sts

Row 3: 1 ch, scBLO to end of row, slst in next empty st of body. 10 sts

Rep Rows 2 and 3 along Front edge until first marker, finishing on a Row 2.

Beg inc at ribbing.

Row 1: 1 ch, scBLO to penultimate st of row, 2 scBLO in last st, slst in next empty st of body. 11 sts – 1 st inc

Row 2: Slst in next st, turn, skip 2 slsts done on body, scBLO to end of row, turn. 11 sts

Row 3: 1 ch, scBLO to end of row, slst in next empty st of body. 11 sts

Row 4: Slst in next st, turn, skip 2 slsts done on body, scBLO to end of row, turn. 11 sts

Rep last 4 rows along neckline shaping, finishing on a Row 2 or 4, inc 1 st of ribbing every 4 rows until next marker at top of neckline. Ribbing stitch count will depend on how many sts were between first and second markers.

Now stop inc ribbing sts, but change rate of work by making 2 rows of ribbing on every row of neckline as follows:

Row 1: 1 ch, scBLO to last st of row, slst in next empty st of body, turn.

Row 2: Skip slst done on body, scBLO to end of row, turn.

Rep last two rows until next marker at other side of neckline.

Beg dec at ribbing and return to making 2 rows of ribbing for every 2 rows of edging.

Row 1: 1 ch, scBLO to last 2 sts of row, sc2tog in last 2 sts, slst in next empty st of body. 1 st dec

Row 2: Slst in next st, turn, skip 2 slsts done on body, scBLO to end of row, turn.

Row 3: 1 ch, scBLO to end of row, slst in next empty st of body.

Row 4: Slst in next st, turn, skip 2 slsts done on body, scBLO to end of row, turn.

Rep last 4 rows along neckline shaping, dec 1 st of ribbing every 4 rows until next marker at bottom of neckline, making sure you finish with 10 sts of ribbing on a Row 2 or 4.

Now stop dec and work ribbing by working foll 2 rows:

Row 1: 1 ch, scBLO to end of row, slst in next empty st of body. 10 sts

Row 2: Slst in next st, turn, skip 2 slsts done on body, scBLO to end of row, turn. 10 sts

Rep last two rows to bottom of Front.

Fasten off.

BOTTOM EDGING

On RS, join A to bottom right corner of Front, 1 ch, rsc to penultimate st of row at left corner of front, slst in last st.

Fasten off.

Finishing

Weave in all ends and block to size.

Fernweh tank top

Fernweh (German) — refers to an ache for distant places, a homesickness for traveling.

See Project Information for finished size dimensions.

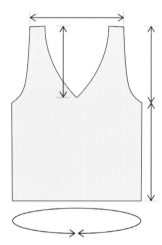

I love this word since I am most familiar with its meaning. The Fernweh tank top is a reminder of those faraway places we are yet to explore, a ladder to something new and different; but also serving as a bridge between our homes and hearts to those adventures that await the wearer. Both panels sport a mosaic motif that, although repetitive, will keep you interested throughout the process of making. The colorful edging brightens an otherwise monochrome background.

SIZES
9 sizes (1–9)

YARN
Knit Picks Lindy Chain (70% linen, 30% Pima cotton), fingering (2ply), 50g (180yd/164m), in the following colors:
A: Black; 1¼ (2, 2, 2½, 3½) (3¾, 4, 5½, 5½) balls
B: Linen; 1¼ (2, 2, 2½, 3½) (3¾, 4, 5½, 5½) balls
C: Serrano; ¼ (¼, ¼, ¼, ¼) (¼, ¼, ¼, ¼) balls

TOOLS
US size G/6 (4mm) hook
US size 7 (4.5mm) hook
5 stitch markers

GAUGE (TENSION)
18 sts x 24 rows measure 4 x 4in (10 x 10cm) over standard mosaic crochet using a US size G/6 (4mm) hook.

SPECIAL ABBREVIATION
mdc, mosaic double crochet: dc in skipped st of same color 3 rows below, working in front of intervening 2 rows of ch in other color

NOTES

Fernweh is worked in two separate identical panels. Each panel is worked bottom-up following charts (see Colorwork Techniques: Mosaic Crochet, Standard Mosaic Crochet).

Before starting the body, choose your desired length and compare it to the minimum length shown in Project Information: Fernweh tank top Finished Sizes table. Then follow the instructions that correspond, depending on whether extra length will be added or not. After the body has been completed, the underarms are shaped by decreasing at each side. The V-neck starts with decreases at the inside of the neck to the strap width. One side of the neckline is striped, the other side continues to follow the pattern in the chart. Once both panels are complete, they are joined at the sides and straps and a colorful i-cord edging is worked around neckline and armhole openings.

Panel

(make 2)

BODY

Using US size G/6 hook and A, make a crochet cord of 67 (75, 85, 95, 103) (113, 123, 133, 143) sts (see General Techniques: Crochet Cord).

Turn, and work on the front loop so Row 1 is on WS.

Row 1 (WS): 1 ch (doesn't count as st throughout), scFLO to end of row, changing to B on last st. The foll row will be a RS row.

Count 33 (37, 42, 47, 51) (56, 61, 66, 71) sts from beg of row. PM in next st to mark middle st.

Notes: First and last 3 (2, 2, 2, 1) (1, 1, 1, 1) sts of row will always be sc in color of row—they are a rep of first and last st of charts 1 and 2A.

If minimum length stated in Project Information: Fernweh tank top Finished Sizes is long enough, start to work from Minimum Length. If this length feels too short, then start with To add More Length.

TO ADD MORE LENGTH

Rep Chart 1 as many times as necessary to reach desired length minus minimum length stated in Finished Sizes, finishing on a Row 10.

Cont with minimum length.

TO WORK FROM MINIMUM LENGTH

Start working Chart 2A (Chart 1 is only worked when adding extra length).

If extra length was added, omit Row 0 of Chart 2A and start with Row 1. Otherwise, start with Row 0.

Work Chart 2A once, then rep Chart 2B a total of 0 (1, 1, 1, 2) (2, 1, 2, 2) times.

SIZES 7 (8, 9) ONLY

Work Chart 2B once more and start shaping the underarm on Chart 2B Row 19 (15, 13). After last row of Chart 2B, work sc to marker, then work Chart 3 after marked st whilst cont to shape underarm.

SIZES 1 (2, 3, 4, 5) (6) ONLY

After last row of Chart 2B, work sc to marker and then work Chart 3 after marked st. At same time start shaping underarm on Chart 3 Row 9 (9, 9, 9, 3) (1).

Chart 1

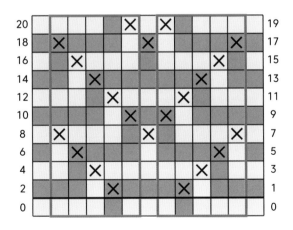

KEY

| ■ | A | □ | B | **X** | mosaic double crochet (mdc) |

This chart only to be worked if adding extra length to minimum length stated in Finished Sizes.

Work from bottom up, right to left on RS (odd-number) rows, left to right on WS (even-number) rows. Each square represents one st and each chart row represents 2 rows of crochet.

Chart follows all Standard Mosaic Crochet rules (see Colorwork Techniques: Mosaic Crochet).

Rep first and last st of chart on first and last 3 (2, 2, 2, 1) (1, 1, 1, 1) sts of row.

Rep first portion in red until before middle st. Then rep second portion in red until 3 (2, 2, 2, 1) (1, 1, 1, 1) sts from end of row.

Row 0 is to only be worked once and not rep again.

Chart 2A

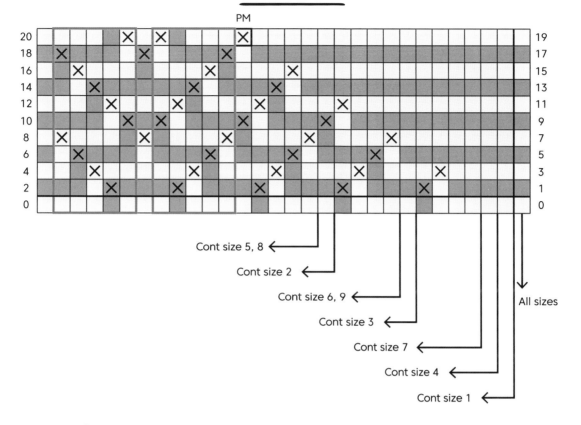

PM

Cont size 5, 8 ←

Cont size 2 ←

Cont size 6, 9 ←

Cont size 3 ←

Cont size 7 ←

Cont size 4 ←

Cont size 1 ←

All sizes

KEY

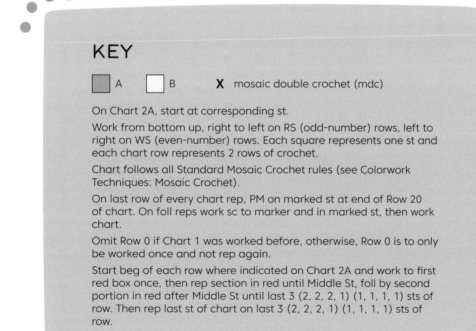

A   B   **X** mosaic double crochet (mdc)

On Chart 2A, start at corresponding st.

Work from bottom up, right to left on RS (odd-number) rows, left to right on WS (even-number) rows. Each square represents one st and each chart row represents 2 rows of crochet.

Chart follows all Standard Mosaic Crochet rules (see Colorwork Techniques: Mosaic Crochet).

On last row of every chart rep, PM on marked st at end of Row 20 of chart. On foll reps work sc to marker and in marked st, then work chart.

Omit Row 0 if Chart 1 was worked before, otherwise, Row 0 is to only be worked once and not rep again.

Start beg of each row where indicated on Chart 2A and work to first red box once, then rep section in red until Middle St, foll by second portion in red after Middle St until last 3 (2, 2, 2, 1) (1, 1, 1, 1) sts of row. Then rep last st of chart on last 3 (2, 2, 2, 1) (1, 1, 1, 1) sts of row.

PM on last st prior to first red box on Rows 19 and 20.

When rep Chart 2B, work sc in color of row until marker, then work each row of Chart 2B from beg.

Chart 2B

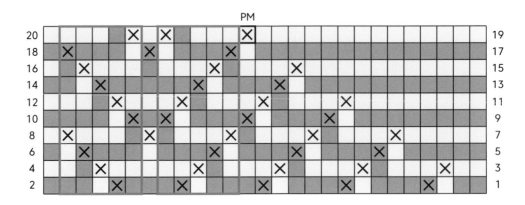

Chart 3

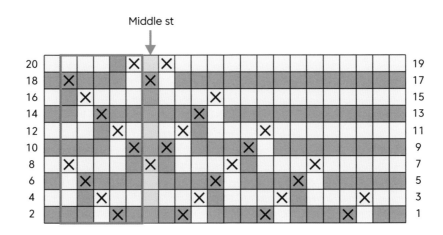

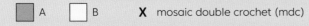

KEY

■ A   □ B   **X** mosaic double crochet (mdc)

Work from bottom up, right to left on RS (odd-number) rows, left to right on WS (even-number) rows. Each square represents one st and each chart row represents 2 rows of crochet.

Charts follow all Standard Mosaic Crochet rules (see Colorwork Techniques: Mosaic Crochet).

Chart 3: Work sc in color of row until marker placed at end of last rep of Chart 2, then work each row of Chart 3 from beg until Middle St, foll by rep portion in red after Middle St. Rep last st of chart on last 3 (2, 2, 2, 1) (1, 1, 1, 1) sts of row.

SHAPING UNDERARM

Row 9 (9, 9, 9, 3) (1, 19, 15, 13) of Chart 3 (3, 3, 3, 3) (3, 2B, 2B, 2B): "Close" first and last 6 (7, 8, 9, 10) (12, 15, 17, 19) sts by omitting all ch-sp sts and making sc instead, foll chart on rest of row.

Fasten off both yarns at end of WS row.

Notes: Remember that each row of chart represents two rows of crochet. From now on, when it says RS and WS next to a row, it means only one row of your work and not of chart.

On sizes 7, 8, 9 only, once Chart 2 is completed, continue following Chart 3.

Set-up row (RS): Skip first 4 (5, 6, 7, 8) (10, 13, 15, 17) sts, join yarn corresponding to next row in chart to next st.

Work chart to last 6 (7, 8, 9, 10) (12, 15, 17, 19) sts, sc in next 2 sts, turn, leaving last 4 (5, 6, 7, 8) (10, 13, 15, 17) sts unworked. 59 (65, 73, 81, 87) (93, 97, 103, 109) sts

Set-up row (WS): 1 ch, sc2tog, work chart to last 2 sts of row, sc2tog, changing color on last st. 57 (63, 71, 79, 85) (91, 95, 101, 107) sts – 2 sts dec

Next RS row: Work chart to last 2 sts of row, "close" last 2 sts by omitting any ch-sp sts and making sc instead, turn.

Next WS row: 1 ch, sc2tog, work chart to last 2 sts of row, sc2tog, changing color on last st. 55 (61, 69, 77, 83) (89, 93, 99, 105) sts – 2 sts dec

Rep prev RS and WS rows 1 (3, 3, 3, 6) (7, 8, 10, 11) more times. 53 (55, 63, 71, 71) (75, 77, 79, 83) sts

SIZE 1 ONLY

Cont working Chart 3 until end of Row 20 without dec at underarm anymore. Then cont with Neckline shaping.

RIGHT SIDE NECKLINE SHAPING

Cont changing color at the end of every WS row.

Row 1 (RS): 1 ch, sc to one st before middle st, sc2tog, turn. 26 (27, 31, 35, 35) (37, 38, 39, 41) sts

SIZES 1 (2) ONLY

Row 2 (WS): 1 ch, sc2tog, sc to end of row, change colors on last st, turn. 25 (26) sts – 1 st dec

SIZES 3 (4, 5) (6, 7, 8, 9) ONLY

Row 2 (WS): 1 ch, sc2tog, sc to last 2 sts, sc2tog, change color on last st, turn. 29 (33, 33) (35, 36, 37, 39) sts – 2 sts dec

SIZES 1 (2, 3) ONLY

Skip ahead to Neckline Decreases Only.

SIZES 4 (5) (6, 7, 8, 9) ONLY

Cont with Neckline and Underarm Decreases, rep foll RS and WS rows for 4 (2) (4, 6, 4, 8) more rows, then move to Neckline Decreases Only. 27 (30) (29, 27, 31, 27) sts

NECKLINE AND UNDERARM DEC

Next RS row: 1 ch, sc to last 2 sts, sc2tog, turn. 1 st dec

Next WS row: 1 ch, sc2tog, sc to last 2 sts of row, sc2tog, change color on last st, turn. 2 sts dec

NECKLINE DEC ONLY

Next RS row: 1 ch, sc to last 2 sts, sc2tog, turn. 1 st dec

Next WS row: 1 ch, sc2tog, sc to end of row, change color on last st, turn. 1 st dec

Rep Neckline Dec Only until there are a total of 7 sts left.

STRAP

*1 ch, sc to end of row, turn; rep from * until desired strap length—approx 7½ (8, 8⅝, 8⅝, 9½) (9⅞, 10⅝, 11½, 11½) in/19 (20, 22, 22, 24) (25, 27, 29, 29) cm from underarm.

Fasten off.

LEFT SIDE NECKLINE SHAPING

Join A to middle st.

SIZES 3 (4, 5) (6, 7, 8, 9)

Work Chart 4 for next 2 (6, 4) (6, 8, 6, 10) rows, dec at neckline on every row and dec at underarm on every WS row as established in Body. Skip ahead to Neckline Decreases Only.

NECKLINE DEC ONLY

Work Chart 4, dec at neckline only until there are a total of 7 sts left. First and last st will always be a sc, 5 sts between should foll patt established by chart.

STRAP

Work with 7 sts to match other strap.

Fasten off.

Chart 4

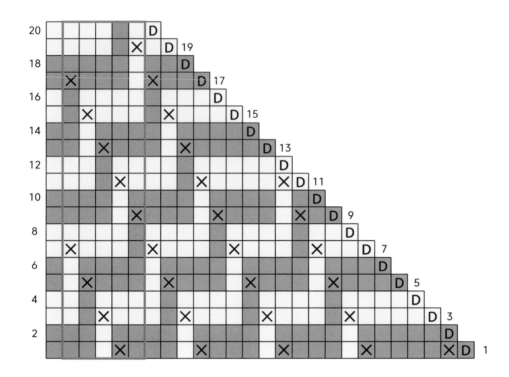

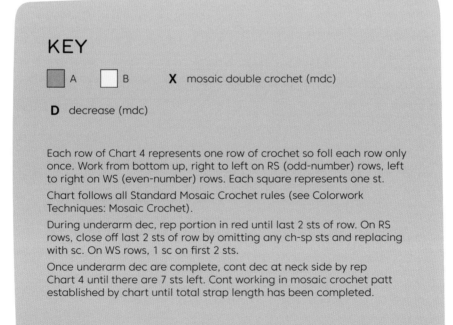

KEY

■ A   □ B   **X** mosaic double crochet (mdc)

D decrease (mdc)

Each row of Chart 4 represents one row of crochet so foll each row only once. Work from bottom up, right to left on RS (odd-number) rows, left to right on WS (even-number) rows. Each square represents one st.

Chart follows all Standard Mosaic Crochet rules (see Colorwork Techniques: Mosaic Crochet).

During underarm dec, rep portion in red until last 2 sts of row. On RS rows, close off last 2 sts of row by omitting any ch-sp sts and replacing with sc. On WS rows, 1 sc on first 2 sts.

Once underarm dec are complete, cont dec at neck side by rep Chart 4 until there are 7 sts left. Cont working in mosaic crochet patt established by chart until total strap length has been completed.

Finishing

Place both panels RS tog. Sew sides of body and ends of shoulder straps using tapestry needle and scrap piece of yarn.

NECKLINE EDGING

Using US size 7 hook join C to a shoulder seam at neckline edge, sc around neckline until one st before middle of V at Front, sc2tog to join each side of V, skipping space in middle. Cont to sc around to beg of row at shoulder, rep the sc2tog at Back V, do not join round but cont working in spiral.

Faux i-cord edging: PM in first st to mark beg of round, BPsc around twice, slst in first st to join round

Fasten off.

ARMHOLE EDGING

Using US size 7 hook join C to middle of underarm, sc around opening until beg of round, do not join round but cont working in spiral.

Work faux i-cord edging as for neckline edging.

Rep on other side.

Weave in all ends and block to measurements.

Lagom pullover

Lagom (Swedish) — refers to something that is just the right amount. In Sweden, it also represents the idea of living a balanced life.

See Project Information for finished size dimensions.

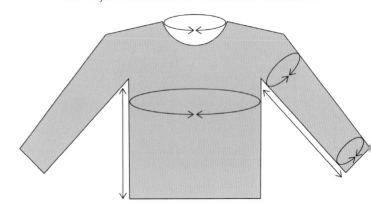

SIZES
9 sizes (1-9)

YARN
The Fiber Co Canopy Fingering (50% alpaca, 30% merino wool, 20% bamboo), fingering (2ply), 50g (200yd/183m), in the following colors:

A: Macaw; 1 (1, 1¼, 1¼, 1½) (1½, 1¾, 1¾, 2)
B: Fern; 1 (1, 1, 1, 1¼) (1¼, 1¼, 1½, 1½)
C: Sarsaparilla; 1 (1, 1, 1, 1) (1¼, 1¼, 1½, 1½)
D: Dragonfruit; 1 (1, 1¼, 1¼, 1½) (1½, 1¾, 1¾, 2)
E: Wild Ginger; 5½ (6¼, 7, 7¾, 8½) (9¼, 10, 11, 11½)

TOOLS
US size E/4 (3.5mm) crochet hook
US size G/6 (4mm) crochet hook

GAUGE (TENSION)
21 sts x 24 rounds = 4 x 4in (10 x 10cm) over chart using a US size E/4 (3.5mm) hook.
21 sts x 16 rounds = 4 x 4in (10 x 10cm) over body patt (1 row sc, 1 row dcBLO in the round) using a US size E/4 (3.5mm) hook.

The Lagom pullover is designed to embody the idea of balance, with its vertical and horizontal stripes. It is a round-yoke pullover worked with single-row mosaic crochet as well as in stripes. The pattern is worked in five different colors, but it can be worked in as many as you like.

NOTES

The pullover starts at the top with a faux i-cord neckline, then short rows are worked at the back of the neck for a better fit around neck and shoulders. The yoke is worked in rounds using the chart and written instructions, while at the same time three increase rows are made. Once the yoke is complete, the body is separated from the sleeves and worked to the desired length. The sleeves are then worked. Both body and sleeves end with a faux i-cord edging to mirror the neckline.

The body length is for a cropped jumper. Add 6in (15cm) for a full-length pullover.

Main body

NECKLINE

Using US size G/6 hook and A, ch 89 (95, 107, 113, 125) (131, 137, 140, 146), slst in first ch to make a ring.

Make 5-row faux i-cord neckline as foll:

Round 1: 1 ch (does not count as a st), 1 sc in each ch around. Do not join round, cont in spiral.

Round 2: BPsc around, PM in first st to mark beg of round.

Repeat last round 3 more times.

Change to US size E/4 hook.

Finishing round (RS): Join last round to starting ch by working sc in BLO of sts on last round and unused loop of starting ch tog around, slst in first st to join. 89 (95, 107, 113, 125) (131, 137, 140, 146) sts

SHORT ROWS

Row 1 will go to one side, inc twice, turn; Row 2 will return to center of back without inc, then cont on to other side, inc twice, and turn. Row 3 will return to center of back again and close round. Use invisible join to join short row rounds.

Row 1 (RS): 1 ch (doesn't count as a st throughout), 12 (13, 15, 16, 18) (19, 20, 21, 22) sc, PM in first st to mark beg of round, 2 sc in next st, PM in first st of inc, 11 (12, 14, 15, 17) (18, 19, 19, 20) sc, 2 sc in next st, PM in second st of inc, 5 sc, turn. 32 (34, 38, 40, 44) (46, 48, 49, 51) sts

Row 2 (WS): 1 ch, skip first st, sc to beg of round passing all markers, 1 sc in beg of round, PM, 1 ch (does not count as a st), 12 (13, 15, 16, 18) (19, 20, 21, 22) sc, 2 sc in next st, PM in first st of

inc, 11 (12, 14, 15, 17) (18, 19, 19, 20) sc, 2 sc in next st, PM in second st of inc, 5 sc, turn. [63 (67, 75, 79, 87) (91, 95, 97, 101) sts]

Row 3 (RS): 1 ch, skip first st, sc to beg of round passing all markers, slst in beg of round to join. 31 (33, 37, 39, 43) (45, 47, 48, 50) sts

First set of short rows completed.

Row 4 (RS): 1 ch, 1 sc in first st (beg of round), PM, *sc to marker, 2 sc in marked st*, PM in first st of inc, rep from * to *, PM in second st of inc, sc to "step" left at end of prev short row, 1 sc in "step", 1 sc in next 3 sts of neck, turn. 37 (39, 43, 45, 49) (51, 53, 54, 56) sts

Row 5 (WS): 1 ch, skip first st, sc to beg of round passing all markers, 1 sc in beg of round and PM, 1 ch (does not count as a st), *sc to marker, 2 sc in marked st*, PM in first st of inc, rep from * to *, PM in second st of inc, sc to "step" left at end of prev short row, 1 sc in "step", 1 sc in next 3 sts of neck, turn. 73 (77, 85, 89, 97) (101, 105, 107, 111) sts

Row 6 (RS): 1 ch, skip first st, sc to beg of round passing all markers, slst in beg of round to join. 36 (38, 42, 44, 48) (50, 52, 53, 55) sts

Second set of short rows completed.

Rep Rows 4 to 6 twice more.

There are now 46 (48, 52, 54, 58) (60, 62, 63, 65) sts at each side of Center Back seam; a total of 105 (111, 123, 129, 141) (147, 153, 156, 162) sts around neck incl 92 (96, 104, 108, 116) (120, 124, 126, 130) sts at Back, 2 short row steps, and 11 (13, 17, 19, 23) (25, 27, 28, 30) unworked neck sts at Front (a total of 16 sts inc around).

Remove all markers.

YOKE

Beg working in rounds on RS only, around whole neck. Yoke has three inc rounds, with single-row mosaic crochet and stripes motif between. Work in "steps" formed by short rows as in normal st.

Change to B.

SIZES 1 (2, 3, 4, 5) ONLY

Inc round 1: 1 ch (does not count as a st throughout), [2 sc, inc1] 5 (5, 5, 2, 2) times, [1 sc, inc1] 39 (42, 48, 60, 66) times to last 12 (12, 12, 3, 3) sts, [2 sc, inc1] 4 (4, 4, 1, 1) times, slst in first st to join. 153 (162, 180, 192, 210) sts

SIZE 6 ONLY

Inc round 1: 1 ch (does not count as a st throughout), *inc1, [1 sc, inc1] twice, rep from * 4 more times, [1 sc, inc1] 51 times to last 20 sts, **inc1, [1 sc, inc1] twice, rep from ** 3 more times, slst in first st to join. 225 sts

SIZE 7 ONLY

Inc round 1: 1 ch (does not count as a st throughout), *inc1, [1 sc, inc1] 4 times, rep from * twice more, **inc1, [1 sc, inc1] 5 times, rep from ** 8 more times to last 27 sts, ***inc1, [1 sc, inc1] 4 times, rep from *** twice more, slst in first st to join. 237 sts

SIZE 8 ONLY

Inc round 1: 1 ch (does not count as a st throughout), *inc1, [1 sc, inc1] twice, [inc1, (1 sc, inc1) 3 times] 3 times, rep from * 5 more times, slst in first st to join. 246 sts

SIZE 9 ONLY

Inc round 1: 1 ch (does not count as a st throughout), [1 sc, inc1] 3 times, *inc1, [1 sc, inc1] twice, rep from * 29 more times to last 6 sts, [1 sc, inc1] 3 times, slst in first st to join. 258 sts

ALL SIZES

Now foll Mosaic crochet chart, using B as color 1 and C as color 2, for next 4 (6, 6, 8, 8) (10, 10, 10, 12) rounds, finishing on a Chart Row 1.

Change to D.

Next round: 1 ch, scBLO around, slst in first st to join.

Rep prev round 2 (2, 2, 2, 2) (2, 4, 4, 4) more times.

Change to E.

On further inc rounds, all inc1 are worked in BLO.

SIZES 1 (2, 3, 4, 5) ONLY

Inc round 2: 1 ch, [3 scBLO, inc1] 5 (5, 5, 2, 6) times, [2 scBLO, inc1] 39 (42, 48, 60, 54) times to last 16 (16, 16, 4, 24) sts, [3 scBLO, inc1] 4 (4, 4, 1, 6) times, slst in first st to join. 201 (213, 237, 255, 276) sts

SIZE 6 ONLY

Inc round 2: 1 ch, [1 scBLO, inc1] 5 times, [2 scBLO, inc1] 69 times to last 8 sts, [1 scBLO, inc1] 4 times, slst in first st to join. 303 sts

SIZE 7 ONLY

Inc round 2: 1 ch, *1 scBLO, inc1, [2 scBLO, inc1] 4 times, rep from * 5 more times, **1 scBLO, inc1, [2 scBLO, inc1] 5 times, rep from ** 8 more times, slst in first st to join. 321 sts

SIZE 8 ONLY

Inc round 2: 1 ch, [1 scBLO, inc1] 3 times, *1 scBLO, inc1, [2 scBLO, inc1] twice, rep from * 29 more times, slst in first st to join. 339 sts

SIZE 9 ONLY

Inc round 2: 1 ch, [2 scBLO, inc1] 3 times, *1 scBLO, inc1, [2 scBLO, inc1] twice, rep from * 29 more times to last 9 sts, (2 scBLO, inc1) 3 times, slst in first st to join the round. 354 sts

ALL SIZES

Next round: Change to C, 1 ch, scBLO around, slst in first st to join.

Now foll Mosaic crochet chart, using C as Color 1 and A as Color 2, for next 6 (6, 8, 10, 12) (12, 14, 16, 16) rows, finishing on a Chart Row 1.

Next round: Change to B, 1 ch, scBLO around, slst in first st to join.

SIZES 1 (-, 3, 4, 5) ONLY

Inc round 3: 1 ch, [4 scBLO, inc1] 5 (-, 5, 2, 0) times, [3 scBLO, inc1] 39 (-, 48, 60, 69) times to last 20 (-, 20, 5, 0) sts, [4 scBLO, inc1] 4 (-, 4, 1, 0) times, slst in first st to join. 249 (-, 294, 318, 345) sts

SIZE 2 ONLY

Inc round 3: 1 ch, [2 scBLO, inc1] twice, [3 scBLO, inc1] 51 times to last 3 sts, 2 scBLO, inc1, slst in first st to join. 267 sts

SIZE 6 ONLY

Inc round 3: 1 ch, [2 scBLO, inc1] 5 times, [3 scBLO, inc1] 69 times to last 12 sts, [2 scBLO, inc1] 4 times, slst in first st to join. 381 sts

SIZE 7 ONLY

Inc round 3: 1 ch, *2 scBLO, inc1, [3 scBLO, inc1] 4 times, rep from * 5 more times, **2 scBLO, inc1, [3 scBLO, inc1] 5 times, rep from ** 8 more times, slst in first st to join. 405 sts

SIZE 8 ONLY

Inc round 3: 1 ch, [3 scBLO, inc1] 6 times, *2 scBLO, inc1 [3 scBLO, inc1] 3 times, rep from * 20 more times, slst in first st to join. 429 sts

SIZE 9 ONLY

Inc round 3: 1 ch, [3 scBLO, inc1] 3 times, *2 scBLO, inc1, [3 scBLO, inc1] twice, rep from * 29 more times to last 12 sts, [3 scBLO, inc1] 3 times, slst in first st to join. 450 sts

ALL SIZES

Next round: Change to D, 1 ch, scBLO around, slst in first st to join.

Now foll Mosaic crochet chart, using D as Color 1 and E as Color 2, for next 10 (14, 16, 18, 20) (22, 24, 24, 25) rows, finishing on a Chart Row 1.

Next round: Change to B, 1 ch, scBLO around, slst in first st to join.

Rep prev round once more.

Next round: Change to E, 1 ch, scBLO around, slst in first st to join.

Sleeves

Now foll Mosaic crochet chart, using E as Color 1 and C as Color 2, for next 4 (4, 4, 6) (6, 6, 8, 10) rows, finishing on a Chart Row 1.

Separate body and sleeves:

Next round: Change to A, 1 ch, 37 (41, 46, 49, 54) (59, 63, 67, 72) scBLO (Back), 11 (12, 13, 15, 16) (17, 19, 20, 21) ch for first underarm, skip 50 (51, 55, 60, 64) (71, 76, 80, 81) sts (First Sleeve), 75 (83, 92, 100, 109) (121, 127, 135, 144) scBLO (Front), 11 (12, 13, 15, 16) (17, 19, 20, 21) ch for second underarm, skip 50 (51, 55, 60, 64) (71, 76, 80, 81) sts (Second Sleeve), 1 scBLO in each st to end of round, slst in first st to join. 171 (189, 210, 228, 249) (273, 291, 309, 330) sts incl underarm ch

BODY

Round 1: 2 ch (does not count as a st throughout), dcBLO around, slst in first st to join. 171 (189, 210, 228, 249) (273, 291, 309, 330) sts

Round 2: 1 ch, sc around, slst in first st to join.

Round 3: Change to E, 1 ch, scBLO around, slst in first st to join.

Now foll Mosaic crochet chart, using E as Color 1 and B as Color 2, for next 8 rows, finishing on a Chart Row 1.

Continue with E for rest of body.

Round 12: 1 ch, scBLO around, slst in first st to join.

Round 13: 2 ch, dcBLO around, slst in first st to join.

Round 14: 1 ch, sc around, slst in first st to join.

Round 15: 2 ch, dcBLO around, slst in first st to join.

Round 16: 1 ch, skip first st, sc to last st, 2 sc in last st, slst in first st to join.

Rounds 13 to 16 set patt. Round 16 avoids seam leaning sideways, but st count remains constant. Cont working in patt until desired length minus ⅜in (1cm), or approx 11 (10¼, 9⅞, 9¼, 8½) (8, 7, 7, 6¼) in/28 (26, 25, 23.5, 21.5) (20.5, 18, 18, 16) cm from underarm, finishing on a Round 13 or 15.

BOTTOM EDGING

Change to US size G/6 hook.

Make 5 round faux i-cord edging as foll:

Round 1: 1 ch, sc around, do not join round but cont working in spiral.

Round 2: BPsc around, PM in first st to mark beg of round.

Rep prev round 3 more times.

Fasten off with invisible join.

With US size E/4 hook again, attach A to middle of underarm to work on RS on unused loops of starting ch.

Set-up round: 1 sc in each ch to end of underarm, 1 scBLO in each yoke sleeve st, 1 sc in each ch to end of round, slst in first st to join. Approx 61 (63, 68, 75, 80) (88, 95, 100, 102) sts

Note: Work sc2tog in corners where yoke meets underarm to close any gaps if necessary.

Round 1: 2 ch, dcBLO around, slst in first st to join.

Round 2: 1 ch, sc around, slst in first st to join.

Round 3: Change to E, 1 ch, scBLO around, slst in first st to join.

Now foll Mosaic crochet chart, using E as Color 1 and B as Color 2, for next 8 rows, finishing on a Chart Row 1.

Note: if sleeve has a number of sts not divisible by three, last rep of chart won't fit completely but disparity will be hidden on underside of sleeve.

Cont in E for rest of sleeve.

Round 12: 1 ch, scBLO around, slst in first st to join.

Mosaic crochet chart

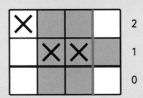

KEY

▨ Color 1   ☐ Color 2

X Double crochet in the front loop only (dcFLO) worked in the stitch 2 rows down

Read the chart from bottom to top, right to left. Row 0 is only worked once on first rep and omitted on foll reps, and the column to the right of the red line indicates the color to be used on that row and is not to be worked.

Rep each row around, making 1 ch at beg of round and using invisible join to join rounds (see General Techniques: Invisible Join When Working in Rounds).

Each square represents one stitch.

All Single-row Mosaic Crochet rules apply (see Special Techniques: Mosaic Crochet, Single-Row Mosaic Crochet).

Round 13: 2 ch (does not count as a st), dcBLO around, slst in first st to join.

Round 14: 1 ch, sc around, slst in first st to join.

Beg dec to shape sleeve:

Round 15: 2 ch, dcBLO around, slst in first st to join.

Round 16 (dec): 1 ch, skip first st, sc around, slst in first st to join. 1 st dec

Rounds 15 and 16 set dec patt. Cont dec in patt until halfway down forearm, approx 12in (30cm) from underarm, or until sleeve reaches desired circumference for cuff.

Now work Rounds 13 to 16 of Body until desired length or approx 16½ (17, 17, 17½, 17½) (18, 18, 18½, 18½) in/42 (43, 43, 44.5, 44.5) (45.5, 45.5, 47, 47) cm from underarm.

CUFF

Change to US size G/6 hook.

Make 5-round faux i-cord edging as foll:

Round 1: 1 ch, sc around, do not join round but cont working in spiral.

Round 2: BPsc around, PM in first st to mark beg of round.

Rep prev round 3 more times.

Fasten off with invisible join.

Rep for second Sleeve at other opening.

Merak hat and cowl

Merak (Serbian) — the pursuit of small, daily pleasures that all add up to a great sense of happiness and fulfillment.

See Project Information for finished size dimensions.

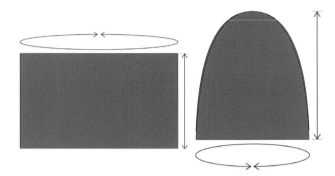

SIZES
Hat: 1 size
Cowl: 2 sizes (S, L)

YARN

HAT
Rosa Pomar Vovó (100% wool), sport (3ply), 50g (156yd/143m), in the following color:
A: color 08; 1 ball
Spincycle Yarns Dyed in the Wool (100% American wool), sport (2ply), 54g (200yd/182m), in the following colors:
B: Ghost Ranch; ½ skein
C: Family Jewels; ½ skein

COWL
Rosa Pomar Vovó (100% wool), sport (3ply), 50g (156yd/143m), in the following color:
A: color 08; 1½ (2) balls
Spincycle Yarns Dyed in the Wool (100% American wool), sport (2ply), 54g (200yd/182m), in the following colors:
B: Ghost Ranch; ½ (¾) skein
C: Family Jewels; ½ (¾) skein

TOOLS
US size G/6 (4mm) hook
US size 7 (4.5mm) hook

GAUGE (TENSION)
19 sts x 18 rows measure 4 x 4in (10 x 10cm) over single-row mosaic crochet chart using a US size G/6 (4mm) hook.

Finding bliss in simple daily tasks can be difficult, but the Merak hat and cowl are a reminder of what it is possible. Despite their simple construction, the results are both beautiful and elaborate. Although the mosaic crochet motifs are easy to follow, the crown shaping on the hat will offer a bit of a challenge. The set is a great introduction to single-row mosaic crochet and the perfect opportunity to get creative with color.

NOTES

The Merak hat is started at the crown, then increases are worked between the mosaic motif. Once the desired circumference has been achieved, the body of the hat is worked in circles following two other charts. At the end, a faux i-cord edging is worked.

The Merak cowl starts with a faux i-cord edging, then two charts are followed around to finish with a matching edging. Both the hat and cowl are worked using A as the main color and interchanging yarns B and C as the contrasting colors for each of the sections and charts.

See Colorwork Techniques: Mosaic Crochet, Single-row Mosaic Crochet for more information on this technique

Hat

Using B, make a magic ring.

Round 1: Using US size G/6 hook, 7 sc in ring, pull on tail to close ring, slst in first st to join round. 7 sts

Use Chart 1 as a supplement to written instructions—rep each row 14 times around.

Work 1 ch at beg of every round and use invisible join technique throughout.

Round 2: Change to A, 1 ch (doesn't count as st throughout), 2 scBLO in each st around, slst to join round. 14 sts – 7 sts inc

Round 3: Change to B, 1 ch, [1 scBLO, 1 dcFLO 2 rows down] around. 28 sts – 14 sts inc

Note: In Round 3 only, do NOT skip sts from prev row behind dcFLO to inc st count. You will need to work 2 dcFLO in each sc st from Round 1.

Round 4: Change to A, 1 ch, [1 dcFLO 2 rows down, skip 1 st, 1 scBLO] around. 28 sts

Round 5: Change to B, 1 ch, [2 scBLO in next st, 1 dcFLO 2 rows down, skip 1 st] around. 42 sts – 14 sts inc

Round 6: Change to A, 1 ch, [1 scBLO in next st, dcFLO 2 rows down, skip 1 st, 1 scBLO] around. 42 sts

Round 7: Change to B, 1 ch, [1 dcFLO 2 rows down, skip 1 st, 2 scBLO in next st, 1 scBLO] around. 56 sts – 14 sts inc

Round 8: Change to A, 1 ch, [3 scBLO, dcFLO 2 rows down, skip 1 st] around. 56 sts

Round 9: Change to B, 1 ch, [2 scBLO, 1 dcFLO 2 rows down, skip 1 st, 2 scBLO in next st] around. 70 sts – 14 sts dec

Round 10: Change to A, 1 ch, [1 scBLO, 1 dcFLO 2 rows down, skip 1 st, 3 scBLO] around. 70 sts

Round 11: Change to B, 1 ch, [1 dcFLO 2 rows down, skip 1 st, 2 scBLO in next st, 3 scBLO] around. 84 sts – 14 sts inc

Round 12: Change to A, 1 ch, [5 scBLO, 1 dcFLO 2 rows down, skip 1 st] around. 84 sts

Round 13: Change to B, 1 ch, [4 scBLO, 1 dcFLO 2 rows down, skip 1 st, 1 scBLO] around. 84 sts

Chart 1

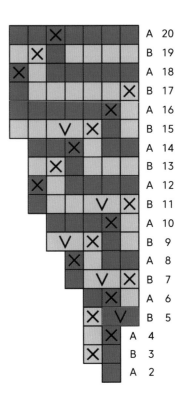

A	20
B	19
A	18
B	17
A	16
B	15
A	14
B	13
A	12
B	11
A	10
B	9
A	8
B	7
A	6
B	5
A	4
B	3
A	2

KEY

 A   B

X double crochet front loop only (dcFLO)

V 2 single crochet back loop only (scBLO)

Chart follows all Single-row Mosaic Crochet rules (see Colorwork Techniques: Mosaic Crochet).

Work from the bottom up, from right to left, each square represents 1 st and each chart row represents 1 row of crochet

Chart 2

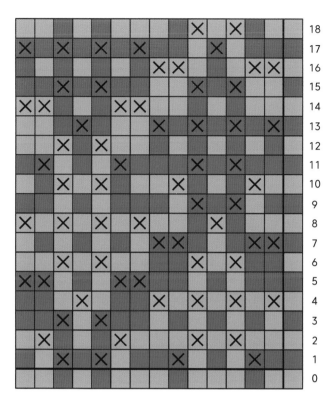

Round 14: Change to A, 1 ch, [3 scBLO, 1 dcFLO 2 rows down, skip 1 st, 2 scBLO] around. 84 sts

Round 15: Change to B, 1 ch, [2 scBLO, 1 dcFLO 2 rows down, skip 1 st, 2 scBLO in next st, 2 scBLO] around. 98 sts – 14 sts inc

Round 16: Change to A, 1 ch, [1 scBLO, 1 dcFLO 2 rows down, skip 1 st, 5 scBLO] around. 98 sts

Note: For a tighter beanie that doesn't slouch, omit foll 4 rounds. Sample worked all 20 rounds.

Round 17: Change to B, 1 ch, [1 dcFLO 2 rows down, skip 1 st, 6 scBLO] around. 98 sts

Round 18: Change to A, 1 ch, [6 scBLO, 1 dcFLO 2 rows down, skip 1 st] around. 98 sts

Round 19: Change to B, 1 ch, [5 scBLO, 1 dcFLO 2 rows down, skip 1 st, 1 scBLO] around. 98 sts

Round 20: Change to A, 1 ch, [4 scBLO, 1 dcFLO 2 rows down, skip 1 st, 2 scBLO] around. 98 sts

Rep each row of Chart 2 a total of 7 times around using A and C, starting with C on Row 0. After working chart once, work Rows 1 to 3 once more.

Work Chart 3 around using A and B, starting with B on Row 0. Stop working chart when desired length of hat has been achieved, making sure to finish on an A (odd numbered) row. Cont with faux i-cord edging.

KEY

 A   C

X   double crochet front loop only (dcFLO)

Chart follows all Single-row Mosaic Crochet rules (see Colorwork Techniques: Mosaic Crochet).

Work from the bottom up, from right to left, each square represents 1 st and each chart row represents 1 row of crochet

Work Row 0 only once at beg.

First column indicates color to be used on that row and row number. It is NOT to be worked.

Work 1 ch at beg of every round and use invisible join technique throughout.

Edging

This edging will tighten brim slightly for a better fit; if you don't wish it to be tighter, use a larger hook.

Using A, scBLO around. Do not join round but cont working in spiral.

Faux i-cord edging: PM in first st to mark beg of round, BPsc around 3 times, slst in first st to join round.

Cowl

Fasten off.

Using US size 7 hook and A, ch 112 (126), slst in first ch to join round.

Set-up round: 1 ch (doesn't count as st throughout), sc around, do not join round but cont working in spiral. 112 (126) sts

Faux i-cord edging: PM in first st to mark beg of round, BPsc around 3 times.

Next round: Change to US size G/6 hook, join last worked round to starting ch with scBLO in sts of last round and unused loop of starting ch around, slst on first st to join round. 112 (126) sts

Work Rows 0 to 9 (11) of Chart 3 around using A and C, starting with C on Row 0. To add extra length to cowl, cont working chart making sure to finish on an A (odd numbered) row.

Work Chart 2 around using A and B, starting with B on Row 0. After working whole chart once (twice), work Rows 1 to 3 once more.

Rep Chart 3, making as many rows as at beg.

EDGING

Using US size 7 hook and A, scBLO around. Do not join round but cont working in spiral.

Faux i-cord edging: PM in first st to mark beg of round, BPsc around 4 times, slst in first st to join round.

Fasten off, leaving a long tail at least twice as long as circumference of cowl.

Finishing

Join last worked round to back of first row of edging by sewing together BLO of sts on last row to back of work using a tapestry needle and tail left after fastening.

Weave in all ends and block to measurements.

Add pompom to hat if desired.

Chart 3

85

Merak hat and cowl

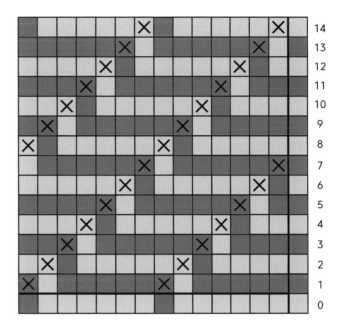

KEY

 A   B

X double crochet front loop only (dcFLO)

Chart follows all Single-row Mosaic Crochet rules (see Colorwork Techniques: Mosaic Crochet).

Work from the bottom up, from right to left, each square represents 1 st and each chart row represents 1 row of crochet

Work Row 0 only once at beg.

First column indicates color to be used on that row and row number. It is NOT to be worked.

Work 1 ch at beg of every round and use invisible join technique throughout.

Pana Po'o summer top

Pana Po'o (Hawaiian) — the act of scratching your head in order to help you remember something you have forgotten.

See Project Information for finished size dimensions.

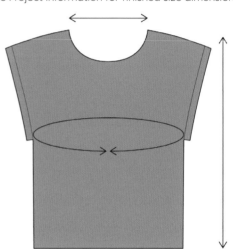

The Pana Po'o summer top symbolizes the crossroads that often make us stop in our tracks and think. It represents endless possibilities and life. The easy construction makes it the perfect introduction to intarsia garments, and although this pattern uses four different colors, it can easily be made with many more.

SIZES
9 sizes (1-9)

YARN
The Yarn Collective Bloomsbury DK (100% merino wool), light worsted (DK), 100g (236yd/240m), in the following colors:
A: Oz (106); 1 (1, 1, 1, 1) (1, 1, 1, 1¼) balls
B: Russet (109); 1 (1, 1, 1, 1¼) (1¼, 1¼, 1¼, 1½) balls
C: Indigo (104); 1 (1, 1, 1, 1) (1¼, 1¼, 1¼, 1½) balls
D: Fuschia (102); 1 (1, 1, 1, 1¼) (1¼, 1¼, 1¼, 1½) balls

TOOLS
US size H/8 (5mm) crochet hook
2 stitch markers

GAUGE (TENSION)
14 sts x 14 rows = 4 x 4in (10 x 10cm) over griddle stitch using a US size H/8 (5mm) hook.

SPECIAL ABBREVIATIONS
griddle st, griddle stitch: alternate (1 sc, 1 dc) throughout, always working sc sts in dc sts from prev row, and vice versa

NOTES

The top is worked in two almost identical panels, each constructed from the top down. The front panel includes neck shaping, which means each side of the neck is worked separately and then they are joined to work the chest and body. Once the panels are complete, they are joined at the sides and shoulders, and an edging is worked around the sleeves. The body length in this pattern is for the semi cropped style, but the length is adjustable to taste.

Front panel

Work neck left side first, then right side.

LEFT SIDE

Make a crochet cord of 9 (12, 16, 19, 23) (26, 29, 33, 37) sts in colors to match Row 1 of Front neck chart starting from neckline as foll:

A: 4 sts, B: 5 (8, 12, 15, 18) (18, 18, 18, 18) sts, C: – (–, –, –, 1) (4, 7, 11, 15) sts.

Change color foll Front neck chart.

Set up griddle st:

SIZES 1 (4, 5) (7, 8, 9) ONLY

Row 1 (WS): 1 ch, 1 scFLO in first st, *1 dcFLO in next st, 1 scFLO in next st; rep from * to end of the row, turn.

SIZES 2 (3) (6) ONLY

Row 1 (WS): 1 ch, 1 dcFLO in first st, 1 scFLO in next st, *1 dcFLO, 1 scFLO; rep from * to end of the row, turn.

ALL SIZES

Cont in griddle st.

Note: When inc1 falls on row end sc, work (1 dc, 1 sc) in same st. When inc1 falls on row beg sc, work (1 sc, 1 dc) in same st.

Row 2 (RS): 1 ch, inc1 in first st, griddle st to end of row, turn. 10 (13, 17, 20, 24) (27, 30, 34, 38) sts

Row 3 (WS): 1 ch, griddle st to last st, inc1 in last st, turn. 11 (14, 18, 21, 25) (28, 31, 35, 39) sts

Rep prev two rows twice then Row 2 once more. 16 (19, 23, 26, 30) (33, 36, 40, 44) sts

Do not fasten off.

RIGHT SIDE

Working with different balls of each color, make a crochet cord of 9 (12, 16, 19, 23) (26, 29, 33, 37) sts in colors to match Row 1 of Front neck chart starting from sleeve side as foll:

C: – (–, –, –, –) (–, –, 1, 5) sts, B: – (–, 2, 5, 9) (12, 15, 18, 18) sts, A: 9 (12, 14, 14, 14) (14, 14, 14, 14) sts.

Change color foll Front neck chart.

Set up griddle st:

Row 1 (WS): 1 ch, 1 scFLO in first st, *1 dcFLO in next st, 1 scFLO in next st, rep from * to end of the row, turn.

Note: sizes 2, 3 and 6 will finish with a dc on last st.

Cont in griddle st.

Row 2 (RS): 1 ch, griddle st to last st, inc1 in last st, turn. 10 (13, 17, 20, 24) (27, 30, 34, 38) sts

Front neck chart

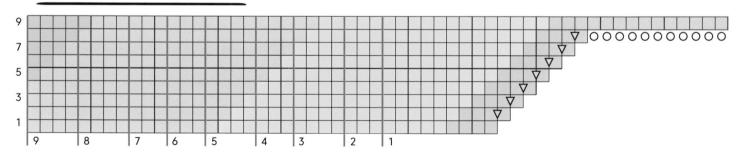

Back neck chart

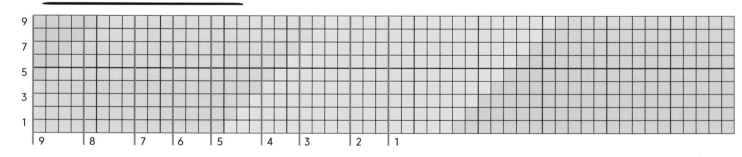

Row 3 (WS): 1 ch, inc1 in first st, griddle st to end of row, turn. 11 (14, 18, 21, 25) (28, 31, 35, 39) sts

Rep prev two rows twice then Row 2 once more. 16 (19, 23, 26, 30) (33, 36, 40, 44) sts

Ch 23, slst in first st of Row 8 of Left Side of neck. Cut A from Right Side ONLY. PM in 12th ch to mark middle st.

Row 9 (WS): Starting where Left Side ended, 1 ch, griddle st to end of row incl ch connecting Right Side of neck to Left Side, turn. 55 (61, 69, 75, 83) (89, 95, 103, 111) sts

BODY

St count will remain constant throughout the Body. Follow Body chart in griddle st throughout until desired length at Front (approx 19¾in/50cm from shoulder corner), moving middle marker up on every row.

When desired length has been achieved, fasten off and cut all strands.

Make a crochet cord of 55 (61, 69, 75, 83) (89, 95, 103, 111) sts in colors to match Row 1 of Back neck chart starting from RIGHT side of chart as foll:

C: – (–, –, –, –) (–, –, 1, 5) sts, B: – (–, 2, 5, 9) (12, 15, 18, 18) sts, A: 50 (53, 55, 55, 55) (55, 55, 55, 55) sts—PM in st number 28 (31, 33, 33, 33) (33, 33, 33, 33) of A to mark middle st—B: 5 (8, 12, 15, 18) (18, 18, 18, 18) sts, C: – (–, –, –, 1) (4, 7, 11, 15) sts.

Change color foll Back neck chart.

Set up griddle st:

SIZES 1 (4, 5) (7, 8, 9) ONLY

Row 1 (WS): 1 ch, 1 scFLO in first st, *1 dcFLO in next st, 1 scFLO in next st, rep from * to end of the row, turn.

SIZES 2 (3) (6) ONLY

Row 1 (WS): Ch1, 1 dcFLO in first st, *1 scFLO in next st, 1 dcFLO in next st, rep from * to end of the row, turn.

St count will remain constant throughout. Follow Back neck chart then Body chart in griddle st throughout until desired length at Back (approx 21⅝in/55cm from shoulder corner), moving middle marker up on every row. Back on sample is about 2in (5cm) longer than Front, but can be adjusted as desired.

When desired length has been achieved, fasten off and cut all strands.

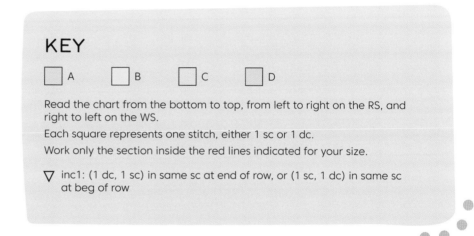

KEY

☐ A   ☐ B   ☐ C   ☐ D

Read the chart from the bottom to top, from left to right on the RS, and right to left on the WS.

Each square represents one stitch, either 1 sc or 1 dc.

Work only the section inside the red lines indicated for your size.

▽ inc1: (1 dc, 1 sc) in same sc at end of row, or (1 sc, 1 dc) in same sc at beg of row

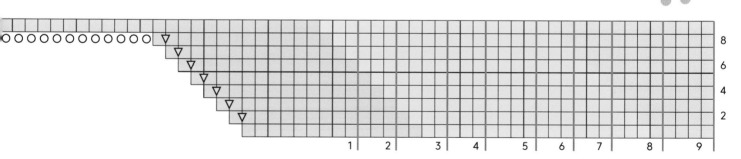

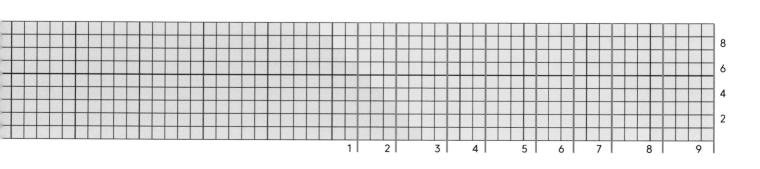

Body chart

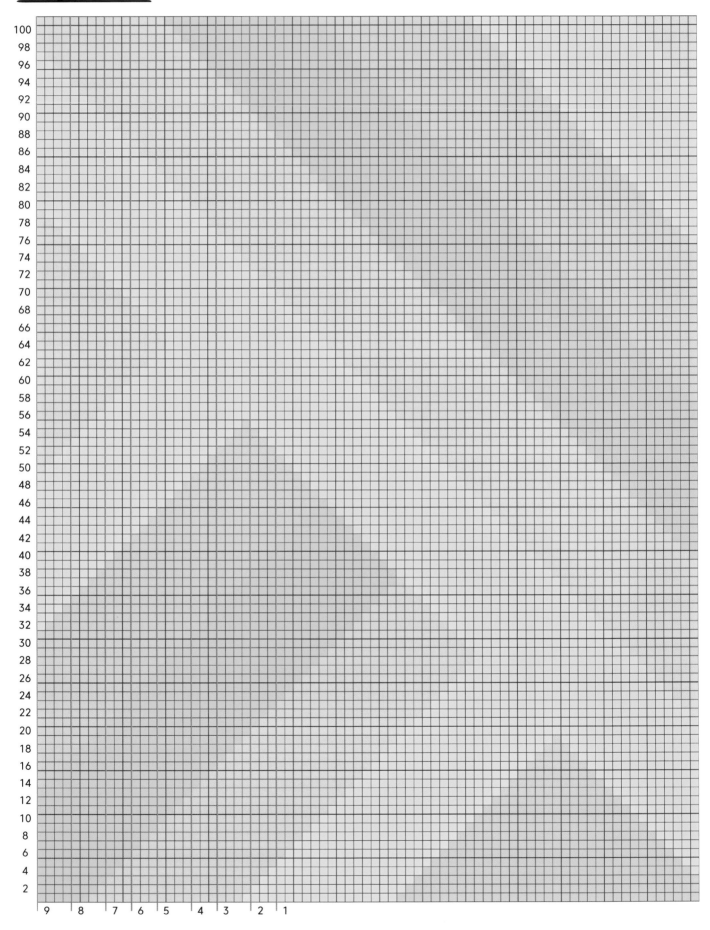

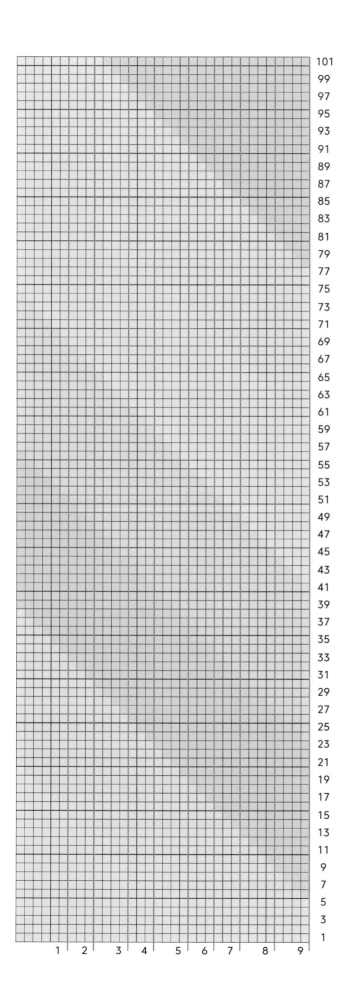

101
99
97
95
93
91
89
87
85
83
81
79
77
75
73
71
69
67
65
63
61
59
57
55
53
51
49
47
45
43
41
39
37
35
33
31
29
27
25
23
21
19
17
15
13
11
9
7
5
3
1

1   2   3   4   5   6   7   8   9

Finishing

Place Back and Front with RS facing and sew together at the shoulders. Measure approx 7½–9½in (19–24cm) down from top corners for the armholes and place a marker on both sides. Adjust the length of the armhole as desired. Sew together from the markers to approx 2in (5cm) from the bottom at the Front.

ARMHOLE EDGING

Attach any yarn color to bottom of armhole.

Round 1: 1 ch, work sc around opening at an approx rate of 5 sts for every 4 rows of griddle st (total number of sts is not important, as long as fabric is not scrunched up or stretched out), slst to join.

Fasten off.

Rep on other armhole.

KEY

A   B   C   D

Read the chart from the bottom to top, from left to right on the RS, and right to left on the WS.

Each square represents one stitch, either 1 sc or 1 dc.

Work only the section inside the red lines indicated for your size.

The chart provided shows all sizes on one chart. You can download individual charts for each size from: www.davidandcharles.com

Gigil cardigan

Gigil (Tagalog) — a situation of such extreme cuteness it's overwhelming, or the irresistible urge to hug something cute.

See Project Information for finished size dimensions.

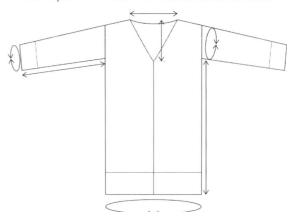

You know that feeling when you see a bunch of puppies playing with ducklings, or a baby's first smile? That's Gigil. This long, oversized cardigan embraces that feeling of cuteness and innocence to its max. With its fun, colorful pattern at the back, this project will help you master intarsia, while at the same time creating a lovely cardigan with a flattering drop-shoulder fit.

SIZES
9 sizes (1–9)

YARN
Sirdar Country Classic Worsted (50% merino wool, 50% acrylic), worsted (aran), 100g (218yd/200m), in the following colors:

A: Milk; 5¼ (5¾, 6½, 7¼, 8) (9, 9¾, 11, 11½) balls
B: Golden; ¾ (¾, ¾, ¾, ¾) (1, 1, 1, 1) ball
C: Moss; ½ (½, ½, ½, ½) (½, ½, ½, ½) ball
D: Oyster; ½ (½, ½, ½, ½) (½, ½, ½, ½) ball
E: Dusky Rose; ¼ (¼, ¼, ¼, ¼) (¼, ¼, ¼, ¼) ball
F: Port; ¼ (¼, ¼, ¼, ¼) (¼, ¼, ¼, ¼) ball
G: Ginger; ¼ (¼, ¼, ¼, ¼) (¼, ¼, ¼, ¼) ball
H: Violet; ⅛ (⅛, ⅛, ⅛, ⅛) (⅛, ⅛, ⅛, ⅛) ball
I: French Navy; ¼ (¼, ¼, ¼, ¼) (¼, ¼, ¼, ¼) ball
J: Fern; ⅛ (⅛, ⅛, ⅛, ⅛) (⅛, ⅛, ⅛, ⅛) ball

TOOLS
US size H/8 (5mm) hook
8 to 12 stitch markers
6 to 10 buttons, ¾in (2cm) diameter

GAUGE (TENSION)
17 sts x 16 rows measure 4 x 4in (10 x 10cm) over double slip stitch BLO using a US size H/8 (5mm) hook.

SPECIAL ABBREVIATIONS
dslst, double slip stitch: yo, insert hook in st, yo, pull through st and both loops on hook
dslstBLO2tog, dslst 2 stitches together through back loops: yo, insert hook in BLO of next st, yo, pull up a loop, insert hook in BLO of next st, yo, pull through st and 3 loops on hook

NOTES

The cardigan is worked in five pieces: back, two fronts and two sleeves—all worked in vertical rows using dslstBLO in the body and slstBLO on cuffs and hems for a knitted rib look. The back has large circles worked following a chart in vertical rows, starting on the left side. Short rows are used to shape the shoulders and back neckline. The front panels are worked from side to middle with seamless pockets, a contrast ribbed hem, and neckline shaping. The left panel has four large circles that intersect with the pocket. Shoulder shaping is done horizontally using short rows. Sleeves are identical and shaped using short rows. All color changes are done using intarsia rules (see Colorwork Techniques: Intarsia Crochet). The fronts and back are joined at the shoulders and the sleeves sewn on. The body side and sleeve seam is then joined on each side. Finally, a ribbed edging is worked around the front openings and neckline.

All ribbed edgings are worked using slstBLO—keep stitches loose so you can work in them on following rows.

WORKING DECREASES
dec2 at beg of row: 1 ch, skip 1 st, dslstBLO2tog, work to end. 2 sts dec
dec2 at end of row: work to last 3 sts, dslstBLO2tog, leave last st unworked, turn. 2 sts dec

Back chart

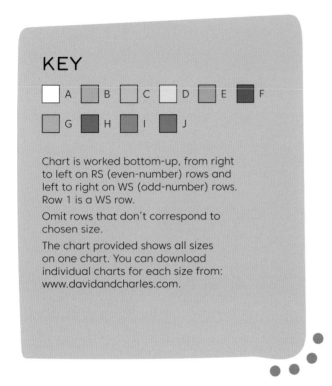

KEY

A B C D E F

G H I J

Chart is worked bottom-up, from right to left on RS (even-number) rows and left to right on WS (odd-number) rows. Row 1 is a WS row.

Omit rows that don't correspond to chosen size.

The chart provided shows all sizes on one chart. You can download individual charts for each size from: www.davidandcharles.com.

Back

Using B, ch 15 for hem, then ch 113 in colors to match corresponding Row 1 of Back chart. 128 sts

Notes: Beg of ch represents bottom of Back, while end of ch is by shoulders. WS rows will be worked DOWNWARD and RS rows will be worked UPWARD. Remember to keep live yarn strands on the WS of your work. This is the back on RS rows and front of WS rows.

Row 1 (WS): 1 ch (doesn't count as st throughout), foll Row 1 of chart in dslst until last 15 sts, change to B and slst to end of ch, turn. 128 sts

Note: Row 1 is a WS row, so move working strands of yarn to front of work underneath hook at every color change to leave strands on WS.

Row 2 (RS): 1 ch, 15 slstBLO using B, foll Back chart using dslstBLO to end of row, turn. 128 sts

Row 3 (WS): 1 ch, foll Back chart using dlsBLO to last 15 sts, change to B, slstBLO to end of row, turn. 128 sts

Rep prev two rows until Back chart is complete. 67 (75, 83, 91, 99) (105, 113, 121, 131) rows.

Fasten off.

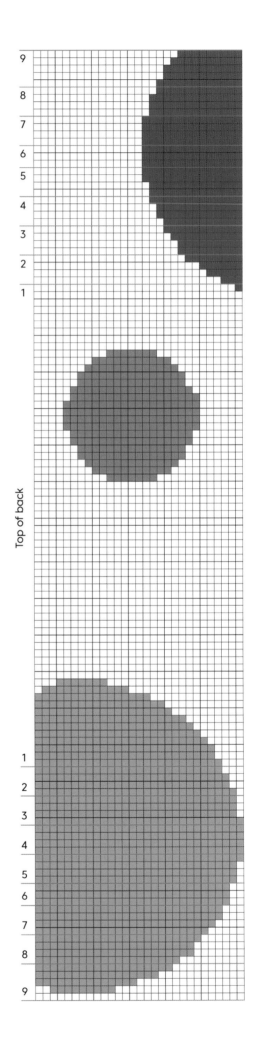

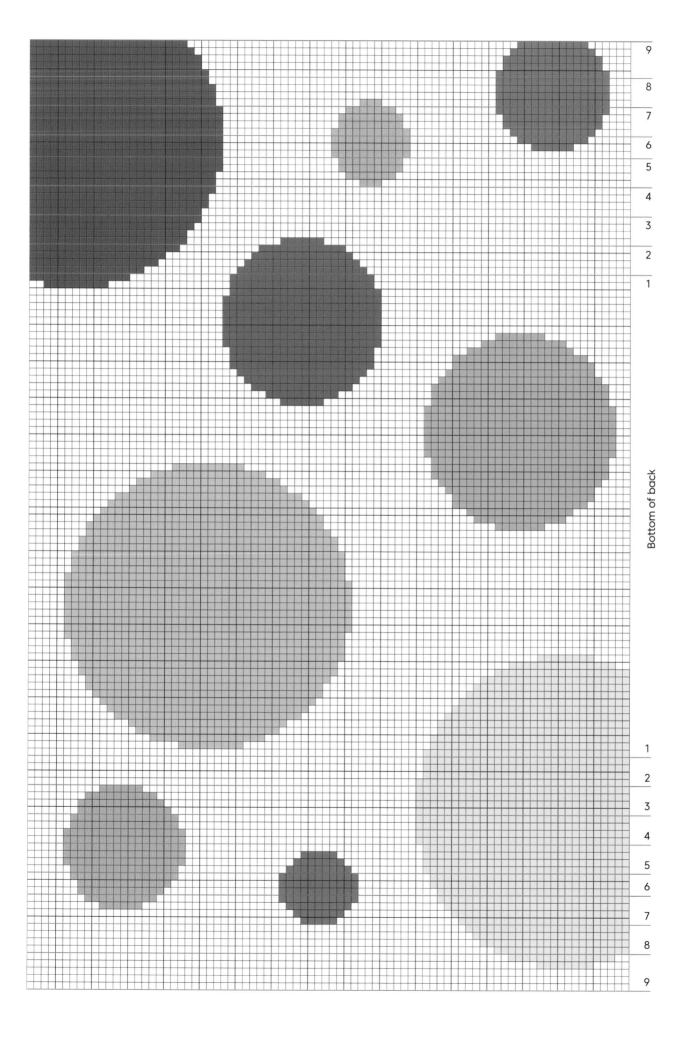

Bottom of back

9
8
7
6
5
4
3
2
1

1
2
3
4
5
6
7
8
9

RIGHT BACK SHOULDER SHAPING

Join A to top right corner on RS.

Row 1 (RS): 1 ch, 1 sc on top of each of next 20 (24, 26, 31, 35) (37, 42, 46, 50) rows, turn. 20 (24, 26, 31, 35) (37, 42, 46, 50) sts

Row 2: 1ch, skip first st, 14 (16, 17, 20, 20) (20, 22, 23, 23) slstBLO, turn. 14 (16, 17, 20, 20) (20, 22, 23, 23) sts

Row 3: 1 ch, skip first st, slstBLO to end of row. 13 (15, 16, 19, 19) (19, 21, 22, 22) sts

Row 4: 1 ch, skip first st, slstBLO to end of last row, slst on step left when prev row turned, slstBLO in next 2 (3, 4, 3, 4) (5, 4, 5, 6) sts, turn. 15 (18, 20, 22, 23) (24, 25, 27, 28) sts

Row 5: 1 ch, skip first st, slstBLO to end of row. 14 (17, 19, 21, 22) (23, 24, 26, 27) sts

SIZES 4 TO 9 ONLY

Rep prev two rows (once, once) (once, twice, twice, twice) more. (24, 26) (28, 31, 35, 38) sts

ALL SIZES

Row 6 (6, 6, 8, 8) (8, 10, 10, 10): 1 ch, skip first st, slstBLO to end of last row, slst on step left when prev row turned, slstBLO to end of row. 17 (21, 23, 27, 31) (33, 37, 41, 45) sts

Fasten off.

LEFT BACK SHOULDER SHAPING

On RS, count 19 (24, 27, 30, 35) (38, 41, 46, 51) rows from left side corner, join A to last counted row.

Row 1: 1 ch, 1 sc on top of each of next 19 (24, 27, 30, 35) (38, 41, 46, 51) rows to corner, do not turn. 19 (24, 27, 30, 35) (38, 41, 46, 51) sts

Fasten off.

On RS, join A to first st of prev row and rep Rows 2 to 6 (6, 6, 8, 8) (8, 10, 10, 10) from Right Shoulder Shaping BUT work in sts from Row 1 FLO and NOT BLO.

Right front panel

Work panels in order set by patt to become familiar with pocket construction without working chart needed for left panel.

Worked vertically from side to center front, with ribbed hem in a contrasting color. First rows are straight and set patt. See Project Information: Gigil cardigan Front Panel Progress Table to determine what to do on each row.

Using B, 15 ch for hem, then using A 113 ch. 128 sts

WS rows will be worked DOWNWARD while RS rows will be worked UPWARD.

Row 1 (WS): 1 ch (doesn't count as st throughout), dslst to last 15 ch, change to B, slst to end of chain, turn. 128 sts

Note: Row 1 is WS row, so move working strands of yarn to front underneath hook at every color change to leave strands on WS.

Row 2 (RS): 1 ch, 15 slstBLO using B, dslstBLO using A to end of row, turn. 128 sts

Row 3 (WS): 1 ch, dslstBLO using A to last 15 sts, change to B, slstBLO to end of row, turn. 128 sts

Rows 2 and 3 set patt.

Work straight in patt for next 3 (5, 7, 7, 9) (11, 15, 19, 25) rows. 6 (8, 10, 10, 12) (14, 18, 22, 28) rows, 128 sts

POCKET

Pocket is started by working top of panel to place where bottom of pocket ends as inside of pocket.

Top set-up row 7 (9, 11, 11, 13) (15, 19, 23, 29) (WS): 1 ch, 68 dslstBLO, 27 dslstFLO, PM on 6th of 27 sts, turn. 95 sts

Cont working straight in patt for 10 (12, 12, 16, 18) (18, 18, 18, 16) more rows. 17 (21, 23, 27, 31) (33, 37, 41, 45) rows, 95 sts

Note: Leave marker on Set-up Row to mark beg of pocket after ribbing.

NECKLINE SHAPING

Row 18 (22, 24, 28, 32) (34, 38, 42, 46) (RS): Work in patt to last 11 (11, 9, 7, 9) (9, 9, 9, 7) sts, dslstBLO2tog, turn. 85 (85, 87, 89, 87) (87, 87, 87, 89) sts – 10 (10, 8, 6, 8) (8, 8, 8, 6) sts dec

Cont to work in patt and AT SAME TIME dec2 at TOP end of every row for 9 (7, 9, 7, 5) (5, 5, 5, 7) more rows (see Working Decreases). 67 (71, 69, 75, 77) (77, 77, 77, 75) sts, 27 (29, 33, 35, 37) (39, 43, 47, 53) rows.

Fasten off A.

FINISH POCKET

Work on bottom of panel to complete hem and outer layer of pocket. Next Set-up Row is worked on same place as previous Set-up Row.

Bottom set-up row 7 (9, 11, 11, 13) (15, 19, 23, 29) (WS): Using new live strand of B, 5 ch, changing to A on last ch. Cont on marked st of prev Set-up Row and dslstBLO on unworked loop left before in next 22 sts incl marked st, dslstBLO in next 18 sts to last 15 sts of row, change to B, slstBLO to end of row, turn. 60 sts

Next row (RS): 1 ch, 15 slstBLO using B, dslstBLO to last 5 sts using A, slstBLO in last 5 sts using B, turn. 60 sts

Prev row sets patt.

Cont working straight in patt for 19 (19, 21, 23, 23) (23, 23, 23, 23) more rows. 60 sts, 27 (29, 33, 35, 37) (39, 43, 47, 53) rows

Fasten off pocket ribbing yarn B only.

CLOSING OFF POCKET AND REST OF PANEL

For next RS (upward) row, place bottom layer of pocket behind outer layer (with prev worked row at front).

Row 28 (30, 34, 36, 38) (40, 44, 48, 54) (RS): 1 ch, 15 slstBLO using B, change to A, 18 dslstBLO, join bottom layer to outer layer of pocket by dslstBLO in each of next 27 sts of both layers, including 5 pocket ribbing sts, dslstBLO to last 3 sts at top of row, dec2, turn. 98 (102, 100, 106, 108) (108, 108, 108, 106) sts

Cont to work in patt and AT SAME TIME dec2 at top end of every row for 3 (5, 5, 7, 9) (9, 9, 9, 9) more rows. 92 (92, 90, 92, 90) (90, 90, 90, 88)

Fasten off.

PM on top st to mark end of neckline shaping.

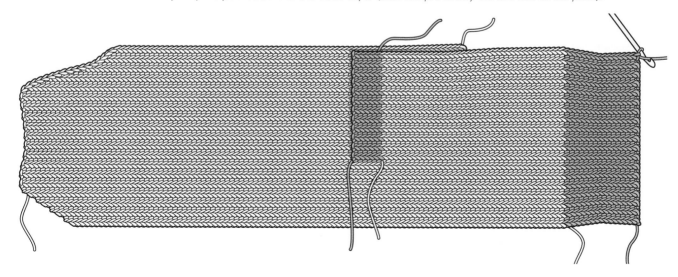

Place the bottom layer of the pocket behind the outer layer (with the previously worked row at the front).

Left front panel

On this panel work all RS rows DOWNWARD and all WS rows UPWARD. Color chart on first 20 rows of panel must be integrated in pocket shaping on both layers.

Using A, 113 ch, using B, 15 ch for hem. 128 sts

Note: Beg of ch indicates top of front, while end of ch is at bottom.

Row 1 (WS): 1 ch (doesn't count as st throughout), slst in first 15 ch using B, change to A and dslst to end of ch, turn. 128 sts

Note: Row 1 is WS row, so move working strands of yarn to front of work underneath hook at every color change to leave strands on WS.

Row 2 (RS): 1 ch, dslstBLO while foll Front chart to last 15 sts of row, 15 slstBLO using B, turn. 128 sts

Row 3 (WS): 1 ch, 15 slstBLO using B, dslstBLO while foll Front chart to end of row, turn. 128 sts

Rows 2 and 3 set patt.

Work straight in patt for next 3 (5, 7, 7, 9) (11, 15, 19, 25) rows. 6 (8, 10, 10, 12) (14, 18, 22, 28) rows, 128 sts

SIZES 8 AND 9 ONLY

Once Front chart is complete, work only using A on body.

POCKET

Work on bottom of panel to complete hem and outer layer of pocket.

SIZES 1 TO 7 ONLY

Cont foll Front chart where it corresponds on foll rows until finished. Once completed, work only using A on body.

ALL SIZES

Bottom set-up row 7 (9, 11, 11, 13) (15, 19, 23, 29) (WS): 1 ch, 15 slstBLO using B, dslstBLO while foll Front chart or using A in next 40 sts, change to new live strand of B, 5 ch, turn. 60 sts

Next row (RS): 1 ch, 5 slstBLO using B, dslstBLO to last 15 sts while foll Front chart or using A, slstBLO in last 15 sts using B, turn. 60 sts

Prev row sets patt.

Cont working straight in patt for 19 (19, 21, 23, 23) (23, 23, 23, 23) more rows. 60 sts, 27 (29, 33, 35, 37) (39, 43, 47, 53) rows.

Fasten off all strands except for yarn B used at hem.

FINISH POCKET

Next row is WS row worked upward.

Identify row before prev Set-up row— Row 6 (8, 10, 10, 12) (14, 18, 22, 28). Join A to 19th st to left of bottom hem on WS at front on unused front loop of st (Bottom set-up row was worked BLO, so front loop is unused).

Top set-up row 7 (9, 11, 11, 13) (15, 19, 23, 29)(WS): 1 ch, 27 dslFLO while foll Front chart or using A as it corresponds, 68 dslstBLO while foll Front chart or A, turn. 95 sts

Cont working straight in patt as set, foll Front chart until finished, then work body using A, for 10 (12, 12, 16, 18) (18, 18, 18, 16) more rows. 17 (21, 23, 27, 31) (33, 37, 41, 45) rows, 95 sts

Front chart

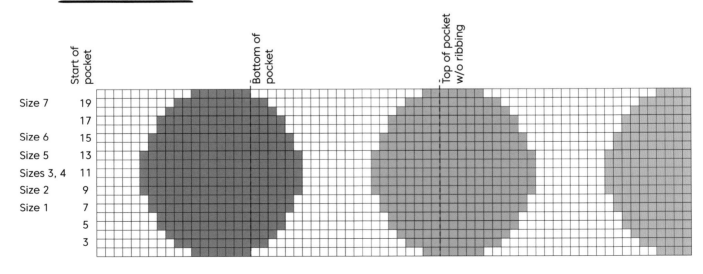

| | | Start of pocket | | Bottom of pocket | | Top of pocket w/o ribbing | |
Size 7 — 19
17
Size 6 — 15
Size 5 — 13
Sizes 3, 4 — 11
Size 2 — 9
Size 1 — 7
5
3

NECKLINE SHAPING

SIZE 1 ONLY

Keep foll Front chart until finished, then cont using A only.

ALL SIZES

Row 18 (22, 24, 28, 32) (34, 38, 42, 46) (RS): 1 ch, skip first st, slst in next 8 (8, 6, 4, 6) (6, 6, 6, 4) sts, 1 ch, dslstBLO2tog (this counts as first st of row), dslstBLO to end of row, turn. 85 (85, 87, 89, 87) (87, 87, 87, 89) sts – 10 (10, 8, 6, 8) (8, 8, 6, 6) sts dec

Cont to work in patt and AT SAME TIME dec2 at top end of every row for 9 (7, 9, 7, 5) (5, 5, 5, 7) more rows. 67 (71, 69, 75, 77) (77, 77, 77, 75) sts, 27 (29, 33, 35, 37) (39, 43, 47, 53) rows.

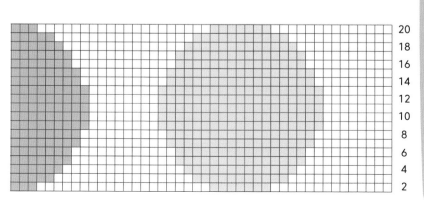

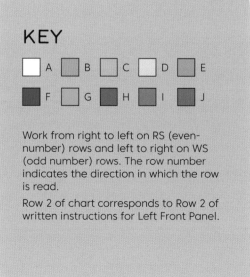

KEY

A	B	C	D	E
F	G	H	I	J

Work from right to left on RS (even-number) rows and left to right on WS (odd number) rows. The row number indicates the direction in which the row is read.

Row 2 of chart corresponds to Row 2 of written instructions for Left Front Panel.

CLOSING OFF POCKET AND REST OF PANEL

For next RS (downward) row, place bottom layer of pocket behind outer layer (with prev worked row at back).

Row 28 (30, 34, 36, 38) (40, 44, 48, 54) (RS): 1 ch, dec2, dslstBLO to last 27 sts of prev row, join bottom layer to outer layer of pocket by dslstBLO in each of next 27 sts of both layers, including 5 pocket ribbing sts, 18 dslstBLO, 15 slstBLO using B, turn. 98 (102, 100, 106, 108) (108, 108, 108, 106) sts

Cont to work in patt and AT SAME TIME dec2 at top end of every row for 3 (5, 5, 7, 9) (9, 9, 9, 9) more rows. 92 (92, 90, 92, 90) (90, 90, 90, 88) sts

Fasten off. PM on top st to mark end of neckline shaping.

LEFT FRONT SHOULDER SHAPING

Join A to top right corner, RS of Left Panel.

Row 1 (RS): 1 ch, 1 sc on top of each of next 17 (21, 23, 27, 31) (33, 37, 41, 45) rows, turn. 17 (21, 23, 27, 31) (33, 37, 41, 45) sts

Row 2 (WS): 1 ch, 12 (14, 15, 17, 17) (17, 18, 19, 19) slstBLO, turn. 12 (14, 15, 17, 17) (17, 18, 19, 19) sts

Row 3: 1 ch, skip first st, slstBLO to end. 11 (13, 14, 16, 16) (16, 17, 18, 18) sts

Row 4: 1 ch, slstBLO to end of last row, slst on step left when prev row turned, slstBLO in next 2 (3, 4, 3, 4) (5, 4, 5, 6) sts, turn. 14 (17, 19, 20, 21) (22, 22, 24, 25) sts

Row 5: 1ch, skip first st, slstBLO to end. 13 (16, 18, 19, 20) (21, 21, 23, 24) sts

SIZES 4 TO 9 ONLY

Rep prev two rows (once, once) (once, twice, twice, twice) more. (23, 25) (27, 30, 34, 37) sts

ALL SIZES

Row 6 (6, 6, 8, 8) (8, 10, 10, 10) (WS): 1 ch, slstBLO to end of last row, slst on step left when prev row turned, slstBLO to end. 17 (21, 23, 27, 31) (33, 37, 41, 45) sts

Fasten off.

RIGHT FRONT SHOULDER SHAPING

On RS of Right Panel count 17 (21, 23, 27, 31) (33, 37, 41, 45) rows from left side corner, join A to last counted row.

Row 1 (RS): 1 ch, 1 sc in top of each of next 17 (21, 23, 27, 31) (33, 37, 41, 45) rows to corner, do not turn. 17 (21, 23, 27, 31) (33, 37, 41, 45) sts

Fasten off.

On RS, join A to first st of prev row and rep Rows 2 to 6 (6, 6, 8, 8) (8, 10, 10, 10) from Left Shoulder Shaping, BUT work sts from Row 1 FLO and NOT BLO.

Sleeves

(both the same)

Using B, 15 ch, change to A, 60 (62, 62, 64, 64) (66, 66, 68, 68) ch.

From now on, RS rows are worked away from cuff (upward) and WS rows are worked toward cuff (downward).

Row 1 (WS): 1 ch, dslst to last 15 sts using A, slst to end of the row using B, turn. 75 (77, 77, 79, 79) (81, 81, 83, 83) sts

Note: Row 1 is WS row, so move working strands of yarn to front underneath hook at every color change to leave strands on WS.

Row 2 (RS): 1 ch, 15 slstBLO using B, dslstBLO using A to end of row, turn. 75 (77, 77, 79, 79) (81, 81, 83, 83) sts

SHAPE SLEEVE

Row 3 (WS): 1 ch, 20 (20, 20, 16, 14) (10, 18, 14, 8) dslstBLO using A, turn. 20 (20, 20, 16, 14) (10, 18, 14, 8) sts

Row 4 (RS): 1 ch, skip first st, dslstBLO to end of row, turn. 19 (19, 19, 15, 13) (9, 17, 13, 7) sts

Row 5: 1 ch, dslstBLO to end of prev row, dslst on step left when prev row turned, dslstBLO in next 20 (14, 14, 12, 10) (8, 6, 6, 6) sts, turn. 40 (34, 34, 28, 24) (18, 24, 20, 14) sts

Row 6: 1ch, skip first st, dslstBLO to end of row, turn. 39 (33, 33, 27, 23) (17, 23, 19, 13) sts

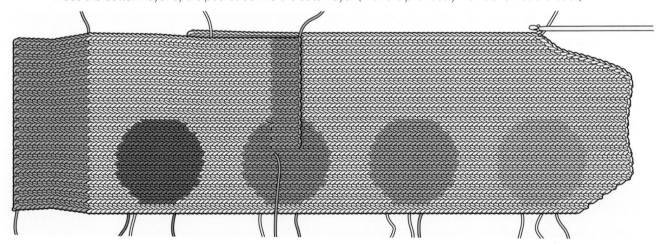

Place the bottom layer of the pocket behind the outer layer (with the previously worked row at the back).

Rep Rows 5 and 6 another 1 (2, 2, 3, 4) (6, 7, 8, 9) more times. 59 (61, 61, 63, 63) (65, 65, 67, 67) sts, 8 (10, 10, 12, 14) (18, 20, 22, 24) rows

Row 9 (11, 11, 13, 15) (19, 21, 23, 25) (WS): 1 ch, dslstBLO to end of prev row, dslst on step left when prev row turned, change to B, slstBLO to end of row, turn. 75 (77, 77, 79, 79) (81, 81, 83, 83) sts

Row 10 (12, 12, 14, 16) (20, 22, 24, 26) (RS): 1 ch, 15 slstBLO using B, dslstBLO using A to end of row, turn. 75 (77, 77, 79, 79) (81, 81, 83, 83) sts

Prev row sets patt

Work straight in patt for 30 (30, 32, 32, 34) (34, 36, 38, 38) more rows. 75 (77, 77, 79, 79) (81, 81, 83, 83) sts – 40 (42, 44, 46, 50) (54, 58, 62, 64) rows

SHAPE OTHER END OF SLEEVE

Short row 1 (WS): 1 ch, 60 (62, 62, 64, 64) (66, 66, 68, 68) dslstBLO using A, turn. 60 (62, 62, 64, 64) (66, 66, 68, 68) sts

Short row 2 (RS): 1 ch, skip first st, dslstBLO to end of row, turn. 59 (61, 61, 63, 63) (65, 65, 67, 67) sts

Short row 3: 1 ch, dslstBLO to 19 (13, 13, 11, 9) (7, 5, 5, 5) sts before end of prev row, turn. 40 (48, 48, 52, 54) (58, 60, 62, 62) sts

Short row 4: 1 ch, skip first st, dslstBLO to end of row, turn. 39 (47, 47, 51, 53) (57, 59, 61, 61) sts

Rep Short Rows 3 and 4 another 1 (2, 2, 3, 4) (6, 7, 8, 9) more times. 19 (19, 19, 15, 13) (9, 17, 13, 7) sts, 46 (50, 52, 56, 62) (70, 76, 82, 86) rows

Last row (WS): 1 ch, *dslstBLO to next step, dslst on step, rep from * until last step, change to B, slstBLO to end of row. 75 (77, 77, 79, 79) (81, 81, 83, 83) sts

Fasten off, leaving long tail to close sleeve and sides of body.

Join A to top right corner on RS along flat shoulder end, 1 sc on side of each row to next corner. 47 (51, 53, 57, 63) (71, 77, 83, 87) sts

Fasten off, leaving long tail to attach sleeve to body.

Finishing

Using mattress stitch, join Front panels to Back at shoulders.

Find middle row of sleeves. With RS tog, place sleeve on top of Back and Front aligning middle row of sleeve with shoulder seam and pin in place. Sew sleeve edging to edge of body using a tapestry needle, keeping it centered.

Note: When attaching sleeves or joining body to edge at last row of the back, make sure to sew in outer loop only to leave front loop on RS intact.

Using tails left at end of sleeve, sew starting ch and outer loop of last row of sleeve tog on WS, then cont with same strand to join sides of body until right before hem. Rep with other sleeve on other side.

BUTTON BAND

Join B to bottom corner of Right Front on RS.

Row 1: 1 ch (doesn't count as st throughout), scBLO along front opening to first marker where neckline shaping starts, 2 sc in marked st, PM on first st, cont to sc along diagonal shaping, sc2tog at corners where Back meets back shoulder shaping, cont to sc to before next marker, 2 sc in marked st, PM on second st, scBLO to bottom of front opening, turn.

Note: When working around neckline, make sure fabric is not being stretched or crumpled. Adjust number of sts per row to make right fit.

Row 2: 1 ch, slstBLO around to next bottom corner, move both markers up in place, turn.

Row 3: 1 ch, slstBLO to before first marker, 2 slstBLO in marked st, PM in first st, slstBLO to before next marker, 2 slstBLO in marked st, PM in second st, slstBLO to end of row, turn.

Row 4: As Row 2.

Mark buttonholes on Right Side Front Panel, making sure they are equidistant and fit between front marker and bottom of hem. Each buttonhole will require 3 sts, so mark middle st.

Row 5: 1 ch, *slstBLO to one st before buttonhole marker, 3 ch, skip 3 sts; rep from * to last buttonhole marker, slstBLO to before first Front marker, 2 slstBLO in marked st, PM in first st, slstBLO to before next marker, 2 slstBLO in marked st, PM in second st, slstBLO to end of row, turn. Remove buttonhole markers.

Row 6: As Row 2.

Rep Rows 3 and 4 twice more.

Fasten off.

Sew bottom of pocket closed on inside of cardigan by joining inner layer to outer layer—do NOT to go through fabric but only sew at back. Sew starting ch of pocket ribbing to 5 unused loops from Set-up Row to match rest of pocket.

Block to stretch button band and bottom hem in place to avoid any scrunching of front and bottom. Add buttons to match placement of buttonholes.

Weave in all ends.

Forelsket shawl

Forelsket (Norwegian) — the euphoric feeling of falling in love at the beginning of a relationship.

See Project Information for finished size dimensions.

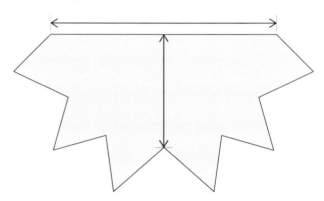

SIZES
1 size

YARN
La Bien Aimee Merino Sport (100% Superwash merino), sport (3ply), 100g (355yd/325m) in the following colors:

A: Peanut Butter and Jelly; ½ skein
B: Liesl; ¾ skein
C: Gateway Purple; 1 skein
D: Waterlilies; 1 skein
E: Life Aquatic; 1 skein

TOOLS
US size G/6 (4mm) hook
16 stitch markers

GAUGE (TENSION)
19 sts x 10 rows measure 4 x 4in (10 x 10cm) over pattern using a US size E/4 (4mm) hook.

SPECIAL ABBREVIATIONS
rsc, reverse single crochet (crab st): 1 ch to start row, *insert hook in next st to right, yarn over (yo), pull through st keeping new loop on hook to left of loop on hook (closer to tip of hook not handle), yo working yarn, pull through two loops on hook; rep from * to last st of row, slst in last st of row

sc-picot, single crochet with a picot: make 1 sc, 3 ch, slst on top of previously worked sc

Remember that euphoric feeling of falling in love, when the lines of where you ended and your paramour started were basically indistinguishable? This is the feeling that Forelsket evokes. The shawl uses striping to create a fade effect that blends colors together, while the striking chevron pattern with lace elements results in a piece that will elevate any outfit. Perfect to keep the chill away, you will want to wear Forelsket all year round. The reverse single crochet makes a beautiful rope-like edging.

NOTES

Forelsket is worked from the top-down, starting at the center of the top edge with a half circle and worked outwards with decreases and increases placed to shape the chevron pattern. Color transitions are worked to achieve the fade effect (see Colorwork Techniques: Stripes and Colorblock). The pattern is set up for four color transitions with five colors. However, the transitions can be done at any time and the effect would be achieved just as well with more or fewer colors. The shawl can also be made larger or smaller than suggested.

Sixteen markers are used to set the pattern. You can learn where they go and omit their use. Otherwise, I recommend using scrap pieces of yarn placed on top of the working yarn right before the marked stitch is to be worked. This is the easiest way to move markers up as you go without having to remove and replace standard markers.

The pattern consists of two rows of double crochet, then one row of 1 dc, [1 ch, skip next st, 1 dc] to end.

shawl

Using A, make a magic ring.

Row 1: 1 ch, 7 dc in ring, pull to tighten ring, turn. 7 sts

Row 2: 1 ch (doesn't count as st throughout), 1 dc in first st, [2dc in next st] 5 times, 1 dc in last st, turn. 12 sts

Row 3: 1 ch, [1 dc in next st, 1 ch, 1 dc in next st] 6 times, turn. 18 sts – st count will include ch from now on

Row 4: 1 ch, dc2tog in first st and next ch-sp, 1 dc in same ch-sp, 1 ch and PM in ch, 2 dc in same ch-sp, and PM in last st, skip 2 sts, *(2 dc, 1 ch, 2 dc) in next ch-sp, PM in first and last dc and in middle ch, skip 2 sts; rep from * 3 more times, (2 dc, 1 ch, 1 dc) in last ch-sp, PM in first dc and in middle ch, dc2tog in same ch-sp and last st of row, turn. 30 sts

Row 5 (inc dc row 1): 1 ch, dc2tog, *(2 dc, 1 ch, PM in ch, 2 dc) in marked ch-sp, dc in next st and PM, skip 2 marked sts, dc in next st and PM; rep from * 4 more times, (2 dc, 1 ch, PM in ch, 2 dc) in marked ch-sp, dc2tog, turn. 42 sts – 12 sts inc

Row 6 (no inc row): 1 ch, dc2tog, *1 ch, skip one st, 1 dc in marked ch-sp, 1 ch, PM in ch, 1 dc in same ch-sp, 1 ch, skip one st, dc in next st and PM, skip 2 marked sts, dc in next st and PM; rep from * 4 more times, 1 ch, skip one st, 1 dc in marked ch-sp, 1 ch, PM in ch, 1 dc in same ch-sp, 1 ch, skip one st, dc2tog, turn. 42 sts

Note: Work in all unmarked ch-sps as in a normal stitch.

Row 7 (inc dc row 2): 1 ch, dc2tog in first st and next ch-sp, dc to before next ch marker, *(2 dc, 1 ch, PM in ch, 2 dc) in marked ch-sp, dc to before next marker, PM in last st, skip 2 marked sts, dc in next st and PM, dc to before next ch marker; rep from * 4 more times, (2 dc, 1 ch, PM in ch, 2 dc) in marked ch-sp, dc to last 2 sts, dc2tog, turn. 54 sts – 12 sts inc

Row 8 (inc dc row 1): 1 ch, dc2tog, dc to before next ch marker, *(2 dc, 1 ch, PM in ch, 2 dc) in marked ch-sp, dc to before next marker, PM in last st, skip 2 marked sts, dc in next st and PM, dc to before next ch marker; rep from * 4 more times, (2 dc, 1 ch, PM in ch, 2 dc) in ch-sp, dc to last 2 sts, dc2tog, turn. 66 sts – 12 sts inc

Row 9 (no inc row): 1 ch, dc2tog, *[1 ch, skip one st, 1 dc in next st] to marked ch-sp, 1 ch, PM in ch, 1 dc in same ch-sp, [1 ch, skip one st, 1 dc in next st] to before next marker, PM in last dc, skip 2 marked sts, dc in next st and PM; rep from * 4 more times, [1 ch, skip one st, 1 dc in next st] to marked ch-sp, 1 ch, PM in ch, 1 dc in same ch-sp, 1 ch, skip one st, [1 dc in next st, 1 ch, skip one st] to last 2 sts, dc2tog, turn. 66 sts

Rows 7, 8 and 9 set patt.

Note: The transition rate and order given is not mandatory. Feel free to foll suggested color patt or transition to other colors when desired and simply cont working in patt until desired shawl span.

Rows 10 to 14: Work in patt using A for another 5 rows, finishing on an Inc dc Row 1.

Rows 15 to 24: Transition to B (see Color Transitions).

Rows 25 to 29: Work in patt using B for 5 rows, finishing on an Inc dc Row 1.

Rows 30 to 39: Transition to C.

Rows 40 to 41: Work in patt using C for 2 rows, finishing on an Inc dc Row 1.

Rows 42 to 51: Transition to D.

Rows 52 to 53: Work in patt using D for 2 rows, finishing on an Inc dc Row 1.

Rows 54 to 63: Transition to E.

Note: If given growth rate there isn't enough yarn to finish transitioning from D to E, end transition after Row 7 and cont using E.

Rows 64 to 66: Work in patt using E for 3 rows, finishing on a No Inc Row.

Cont with Edgings.

COLOR TRANSITIONS

Each color transition is 10 rows long and must be started on a No Inc Row. The color transitions suggested in the pattern are for 5 different colors, but feel free to experiment with color and introduce a new color whenever you want while foll patt. This is the color pattern to foll at each transition (see Colorwork Techniques: Stripes and Colorblock):

Row 1: Fasten off first color and work No Inc Row using second color.

Row 2: Fasten off second color and work Inc dc Row 2 using first color.

Row 3: Work Inc dc Row 1 using first color.

Row 4: Fasten off first color and work No Inc Row using second color.

Row 5: Fasten off second color and work Inc dc Row 2 using first color.

Row 6: Fasten off first color and work Inc dc Row 1 using second color.

Row 7: Fasten off second color and work No Inc Row using first color.

Row 8: Fasten off first color and work Inc dc Row 2 using second color.

Row 9: Work Inc dc Row 1 using second color.

Row 10: Fasten off second color and work No Inc Row using first color.

Fasten off first color and cont in patt using second color.

EDGING

Worked around edge with points.

Cont using E and turn to work along prev row, working in every unmarked ch-sp as a normal st.

Row 1: 1 ch, sc2tog, *sc to before ch marker, (1 sc, 1 sc w/picot, 1 sc) in ch-sp, sc to before next marker, skip 2 marked sts; rep from * 4 more times, sc to before ch marker, (1 sc, 1 sc w/picot, 1 sc) in ch-sp, sc to last 2 sts, sc2tog.

Fasten off and weave in ends. Remove all markers.

TOP EDGING

Worked along straight top edge.

Row 1: Join A to last st of last row, sc along side of every row, at a rate of 2 sc per dc row, to opposite corner, do not turn.

Row 2: Rsc in each st to last st of row, slst in last st of row.

Fasten off and weave in ends.

Finishing

Block to stretch out lace and make sure corners are well defined.

Jayus cardigan

Jayus (Indonesian) — a joke so poorly told and so unfunny that one cannot help but laugh.

See Project Information for finished size dimensions.

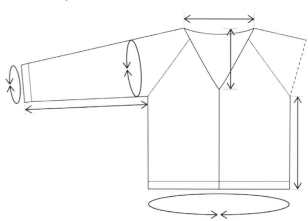

SIZES
9 sizes (1–9)

YARN
Debbie Bliss Baby Cashmerino Sport (55% wool, 33% acrylic, 12% cashmere), sport (3ply), 50g (137yd/125m), in the following colors:
A: Ecru; 3½ (4, 4½, 5, 5½) (6¼, 6¾, 7½, 8) balls
B: Rose Pink; 2¼ (2½, 2¾, 3, 3½) (3¾, 4¼, 4¾, 5) balls
C: Wasabi; 3 (3¼, 3½, 4, 4½) (5, 5½, 6, 6¾)
D: Black; 1½ (1¾, 2, 2¼, 2½) (3, 3, 3½, 3¾)

TOOLS
US size G/6 (4mm) hook
US size 7 (4.5mm) hook
10 stitch markers
6 to 10 buttons, ¾in (2cm) diameter

GAUGE (TENSION)
18 sts x 12 rows measure 4 x 4in (10 x 10cm) over half double crochet using a US size G/6 (4mm) hook.

Jayus embraces the spirit of unlikely matches; the different size color blocks and stripes make a striking effect that keeps the maker and the wearer interested. With this project you can take risks and use bold color combinations, or play it safe with neutrals—you can also use color to accentuate the parts of your body that flatter you the most. It's a beginner-level project with just the right amount of challenge, that will leave you with a fun cardigan perfect to keep the chill away.

NOTES

The cardigan is worked seamlessly top-down with raglan shoulder shaping. The yoke is divided into five sections: two fronts, a back and two sleeves. Increases are worked at the four raglan corners between sections and at the front to shape the neckline. Once the yoke is finished, the body is separated from the sleeves and worked in two sections of different colors (see Colorwork Techniques: Stripes and Colorblock). An edging is worked around the front opening and neckline, finishing with a bottom ribbed hem split at the sides and longer at the back. The sleeves are worked in rounds in the openings left on the yoke, turning at the end of every round for stitch consistency, working narrow stripes throughout, and finishing with a ribbed cuff. The cardigan is completed with a ribbed button band and neckline.

Yoke

Using A, ch 55 (57, 59, 61, 65) (73, 75, 73, 73).

Row 1: 2 hdc in second ch from hook, PM in second st (front marker 1), 2 hdc in next ch, PM in first st of inc (sleeve 1 marker 1), 9 (8, 7, 6, 7) (9, 9, 7, 5) hdc, 2 hdc in next ch, PM in second st of inc (sleeve 1 marker 2), 2 hdc in next ch, PM in first st of inc (back marker 1, 28 (32, 36, 40, 42) (46, 48, 50, 54) hdc, 2 hdc in next ch, PM in second st of inc (back marker 2), 2 hdc in next ch, PM in first st of inc (sleeve 2 marker 1), 9 (8, 7, 6, 7) (9, 9, 7, 5) hdc, 2 hdc in next ch, PM in second st of inc (sleeve 2 marker 2), 2 hdc in last ch, PM in first st of inc (front marker 2), turn. 62 (64, 66, 68, 72) (80, 82, 80, 80) sts

Row 2 (neck and raglan inc row): 1 ch (doesn't count as st throughout), inc1 in first st, *hdc to before marker, inc1 in marked st, PM in second st of inc, inc1 in next marked st, PM in first st of inc; rep from * 3 more times, hdc to 1 st before last st, inc1 in last st, turn. 72 (74, 76, 78, 82) (90, 92, 90, 90) – 10 sts inc

SIZE 1 ONLY

Row 3: As Row 2. 10 sts inc

Row 4 (raglan only inc row): 1 ch, *hdc to before marker, inc1 in marked st, PM in second st of inc, inc1 in next marked st, PM in first st of inc, rep from * 3 more times, hdc to last st, turn. 8 sts inc

Rep Rows 2 to 4 another 4 times. 202 sts

SIZES 2 TO 9 ONLY

For Rows 3 to (15, 16, 18, 20) (21, 22, 23, 26) rep Row 2 another (13, 14, 16, 18) (19, 20, 21, 24) more times. (204, 216, 238, 262) (280, 292, 300, 330) sts

ALL SIZES

PM on first st and last st of row to mark where neckline shaping ends.

Work Raglan Only Inc Rows for next 4 (7, 8, 8, 9) (11, 12, 14, 12) rows. 234 (260, 280, 302, 334) (368, 388, 412, 426) sts – 8 sts inc

SIZES 1 TO 7 ONLY

Hdc in every st without inc for next 1 (1, 1, 2, 1) (1, 1) rows, moving markers up.

ALL SIZES

Note: Before working Separation Row, try on yoke and adjust length for a perfect fit. Add more or remove hdc rows without inc if necessary.

Change to B on last st from prev row and fasten off A.

BODY

Body and sleeves separation row: 1 ch, 31 (37, 40, 44, 49) (53, 56, 60, 64) hdc incl marked stitch, 1 (2, 3, 4, 5) (5, 7, 9, 13) ch for underarm, skip 51 (54, 57, 60, 67) (75, 79, 83, 83) sleeve sts from next marker to foll marker, 70 (78, 86, 94, 102) (112, 118, 126, 132) hdc incl second back marked stitch, 1 (2, 3, 4, 5) (5, 7, 9, 13) ch for underarm, skip 51 (54, 57, 60, 67) (75, 79, 83, 83) sleeve sts from next marker to foll marker, 31 (37, 40, 44, 49) (53, 56, 60, 64) hdc to end of row, turn. 134 (156, 172, 190, 210) (228, 244, 264 286) sts incl underarm ch

Remove all Raglan Increase markers. Leave Front markers where Neck Shaping ended.

St count now remains constant—work on underarm ch as if on a normal st.

Using B, work in hdc rows for 26 rows. Change to C on last st of last row and fasten off B.

Using C, work 20 hdc rows—adjust length if necessary by adding or removing hdc rows using B or C.

Note: Remember to 1 ch at beg of each row (it doesn't count as st).

NECKLINE AND FRONT EDGING

Find raglan inc that flank back neck on starting ch, PM on both starting ch.

From bottom corner where body finished, 1 ch, turn to work along vertical edge of Front where button band and neckline ribbing will go, sc along Front to first marker where neckline shaping starts (approx 3 sts for every 2 rows of hdc), 3 sc in marked st, cont to sc along neckline shaping and starting ch until 2 sts before first Back marker, sc2tog twice, sc to 1 st before next Back marker, sc2tog twice, sc to next front neck marker, 3 sc in marked st, sc to bottom corner at Front. Remove all markers.

Note: Total number of sts in this row is not important, as long as fabric is not too tight so that ribbing doesn't shrink band later on. This row marks RS.

Fold Body so Front is facing up and front opening is centered. PM at bottom corners where body folds to mark where Back separates from Front.

FRONT HEM RIBBING 1

Hem is made with slst ribbing in vertical rows along bottom of Body—leave sts loose to make it possible to work into them and to keep elasticity of ribbing.

Using US size 7 hook and C, ch 12.

Row 1: Starting in second ch from hook, slst to end of ch, when reaching Body, skip first st of last row of Body and slst in next st. 11 sts of ribbing

Row 2: Slst in next st, turn, skip 2 slsts done on body, slstBLO to end of row, turn. 11 sts

Row 3: 1 ch, slstBLO to end of row, slst in next empty st of body. 11 sts

Rep Rows 2 and 3 around bottom edge of body at Front until first marker, finishing on a Row 3.

Sleeves

BACK HEM RIBBING

Row 1: 16 ch, rep Row 1 of Front Hem Ribbing 1. 15 sts of ribbing

Rep Rows 2 and 3 of Front Hem Ribbing 1 until next marker, finishing on a Row 3.

FRONT HEM RIBBING 2

Row 1: 12 ch rep Row 1 of Front Hem Ribbing 1. 11 sts of ribbing

Rep Rows 2 and 3 of Front Hem Ribbing 1 until end of Body.

If finished on a Row 2 cont with Button Band, otherwise fasten off.

BUTTON BAND

PM on edging row for each buttonhole. Check buttonholes are equidistant and fit between end of neckline shaping and end of bottom hem. Adjust number of buttons to taste.

If finished at bottom corner of ribbing, start working vertical rows of ribbing along Front opening and neckline. Otherwise, join C to bottom corner of body at Front.

Using C, ch 8.

Row 1: Starting in second ch from hook, slst to end of ch, when reaching Body, skip very first st of row and slst in next st. 7 sts of ribbing

Row 2: Slst in next st, turn, skip 2 slsts done on body, slstBLO to end of row, turn. 7 sts

Row 3: 1 ch, slstBLO to end of row, slst in next empty st of Body. 7 sts

Rep Rows 2 and 3 around Front opening and neckline, making buttonholes at markers as foll:

Buttonhole row 1: 2 slstBLO, 2 ch, skip 3 sts, 2 slstBLO.

Buttonhole row 2: 2 slstBLO, 3 slst in 2ch-sp, 2 slstBLO.

Cont in patt to next buttonhole marker.

Using US size G/6 hook, join D to middle of underarm.

If last row of Yoke was RS row, make next row on WS and vice versa.

Set-up round: Hdc to end of underarm, around yoke sleeve sts, and to end of round, slst in first st to join round, turn. Approx 52 (56, 60, 64, 72) (80, 86, 92, 96) sts

Notes: Work hdc2tog in corners where underarm meets yoke to close any gaps if necessary.

From now on, turn at end of every round and use invisible join throughout (See General Techniques: Invisible Join).

Read ahead to learn Color and Shaping patts. See Colorwork Techniques: Stripes and Colorblock for more information on color changes and carrying yarn.

COLOR PATT

Work 3 rounds of hdc using D. Work 3 rounds of hdc using A.

Note: Set-up Round counts as one of first 3 rounds of D.

SHAPING PATT

Cont to work color patt while AT SAME TIME, shape sleeve as foll:

Work in color patt for 2⅜in (6cm), then work Dec Round as foll in yarn determined by Color Patt:

Dec round: 1 ch, hdc2tog, hdc around to last 2 sts, hdc2tog, slst in first st to join round. 2 sts dec

Work 5 (3, 3, 2, 2) (1, 1, 1, 1) rounds of color patt without dec.

Rep Dec Round.

Cont shaping sleeves working color patt and a Dec Round every 6th (4th, 4th, 3rd, 3rd) (2nd, 2nd, 2nd, 2nd) round until desired sleeve circumference or until there are approx 6 (8, 9, 11, 14) (18, 20, 22, 22) Dec Rounds worked for a full length sleeve.

Work color patt until desired sleeve length minus 1½in (4 cm) of ribbing; or approx 14¾ (15⅛, 15⅛, 15¾, 15¾) (16⅛, 16⅛, 16¾, 16¾) in/37.5 (38.5, 38.5, 40, 40) (41, 41, 42.5, 42.5) cm from underarm for full length sleeve.

CUFF

Ch 12.

Row 1: Starting in second ch from hook, slst to end of ch, when reaching sleeve, skip very first st of row and slst in next st. 11 sts of ribbing

Row 2: Slst in next st, turn, skip 2 slsts done on Sleeve, slstBLO to end of row, turn. 11 sts

Row 3: 1 ch, slstBLO to end of row, slst in next empty st of sleeve. 11 sts

Rep Rows 2 and 3 around bottom edge of sleeve. On WS, join FLO of each st of last row of ribbing to each starting ch of ribbing with slst.

Fasten off.

Finishing

Block to stretch button band and bottom hem in place to avoid any scrunching of front and bottom.

Add buttons to match buttonholes.

Weave in all ends.

PROJECT INFORMATION

Here you'll find all of the important information regarding yarn yardage/meterage amounts and finished sizes for the projects. Refer to the following tables to identify your size and yarn requirements. Please note that sizes are provided in both imperial and metric measurements.

Commuovere pullover

YARN YARDAGE/METERAGE

Amounts include 10% extra for swatching and margin of error.
Amounts are approximate for a semi-cropped pullover with long sleeves.

SIZE	1	2	3	4	5	6	7	8	9
Yarn A	273½	306¼	328¼	361	383	415¾	437½	459½	492¼ yd
	250	280	300	330	350	380	400	420	450 m
Yarn B	273½	306¼	328¼	361	383	415¾	437½	459½	492¼ yd
	250	280	300	330	350	380	400	420	450 m
Yarn C	1115½	1279¾	1345¼	1476½	1607¾	1728	1782¾	1892	2023¼ yd
	1020	1170	1230	1350	1470	1580	1630	1730	1850 m

FINISHED SIZES

Body length is for full length sweater with long sleeves. Designed with 2–4in (5–10cm) of positive ease.

SIZE	1	2	3	4	5	6	7	8	9
Bust	32½	35⅝	39	42⅛	45⅜	52	55⅛	58¼	64¾ in
	82.5	90.5	99	107	115.25	132	140	148	164.5 cm
Neck	18½	18½	19⅞	20⅞	20⅞	20⅞	21⅝	22¼	23 in
	47	47	50.5	53	53	53	55	56.5	58.5 cm
Upper arm	13	13⅜	14	14¾	16¾	18¼	19⅞	21½	21¾ in
	33	34	35.5	37.5	42.5	46.5	50.5	54.75	55.5 cm
Cuff	8¼	8¼	8¼	8¼	8¾	9	9¼	9½	9¾ in
	21	21	21	21	22.5	23	23.5	24	24.5 cm
Sleeve length from underarm	16½	17	17	17½	17½	18	18	18½	18½ in
	42	43	43	44.5	44.5	45.5	45.5	47	47 cm
Body length from underarm	14⅛	14½	14	13¾	13	12⅝	11¾	11½	10⅝ in
	36	37	35.5	35	33	32	30	29	27 cm

Iktsuarpor tank top

YARN YARDAGE/METERAGE

Amounts include 10% extra for swatching and margin of error.

SIZE	1	2	3	4	5	6	7	8	9
Yarn A	131¼	142¼	153¼	180½	202½	202½	224¼	240¾	251¾ yd
	120	130	140	165	185	185	205	220	230 m
Yarn B	65¾	71¼	76¾	93	98½	104	115	120¼	126 yd
	60	65	70	85	90	95	105	110	115 m
Yarn C	251¾	273½	295½	328¼	350	383	415¾	437½	459½ yd
	230	250	270	300	320	350	380	400	420 m

FINISHED SIZES

Body length is adjustable to taste. Designed with 1–4in (2.5–10cm) of positive ease.

SIZE	1	2	3	4	5	6	7	8	9
Bust	32½	35½	38⅜	44¼	47¼	50¼	56⅛	59	62 in
	82.5	90	97.5	112.5	120	127.5	142.5	150	157 cm
Neck width	6⅞	7⅜	8¾	9¼	9⅜	9⅞	9⅞	9⅞	9⅞ in
	17.5	18.75	22.5	23.5	23.75	25	25	25	25 cm
Neck depth at front	7	7½	7½	7⅞	7⅞	7⅞	8¼	8¼	8¼ in
	18	19	19	20	20	20	21	21	21 cm
Neck depth at back	9	9½	9½	9⅞	9⅞	9⅞	10¼	10¼	10¼ in
	23	24	24	25	25	25	26	26	26 cm
Armhole depth	8¾	9¼	9⅞	10⅜	10¾	11½	11¾	12⅜	12¾ in
	22.5	23.5	25	26.5	27.5	29	30	31.5	32.5 cm
Minimum body length from underarm	9½	9½	9½	9½	9½	9½	9½	9½	9½ in
	24	24	24	24	24	24	24	24	24 cm

Wabi Sabi hat and mittens

YARN YARDAGE/METERAGE

Amounts include 10% extra for swatching and margin of error.

PROJECT	HAT			MITTENS	
SIZE	S	M	L	M	L
Yarn A	109½	120¼	131¼	87½	109½ yd
	100	110	120	80	100 m
Yarn B	87½	93	104	65¾	87½ yd
	80	85	95	60	80 m
Yarn C	93	98½	109½	76¾	98½ yd
	85	90	100	70	90 m

FINISHED SIZES

Hat length is adjustable to desired length.

SIZE	S	M	L
Hat circumference	21⅞	24	26¼ in
	55.6	61.1	66.7 cm
Hat length	9½	9½	9½ in
	24	24	24 cm
Mittens circumference		7	8¼ in
		17.8	21.1 cm
Mittens length		8⅝	9½ in
		21.9	24.1 cm

Ailyak pullover

YARN YARDAGE/METERAGE

Amounts include 10% extra for swatching and margin of error.

For a cropped top with long sleeves.

SIZE	1	2	3	4	5	6	7	8	9
Yarn A	1350	1520	1720	1800	1980	2240	2340	2560	2760 yd
	1235	1390	1573	1646	1811	2049	2140	2341	2524 m
Yarn B	820	920	1040	1090	1200	1350	1410	1550	1670 yd
	750	842	951	997	1098	1235	1290	1418	1436 m

For a full length top with long sleeves.

	1	2	3	4	5	6	7	8	9
Yarn A	1640	1840	2080	2190	2410	2700	2830	3100	3340 yd
	1500	1683	1902	2003	2204	2469	2588	2835	3054 m
Yarn B	1000	1110	1250	1320	1450	1630	1710	1870	2020 yd
	915	1015	1143	1208	1326	1491	1564	1710	1847 m

FINISHED SIZES

Body length is adjustable to taste.

Designed with 1–2in (2.5–5cm) of positive ease.

SIZE	1	2	3	4	5	6	7	8	9
Bust	31¼	34½	37¾	41	46	49¼	52½	57½	62⅜ in
	79	87.5	96	104	117	125	133.5	146	158.5 cm
Neck width	19	19¼	19¼	19⅞	21¼	21¼	21¼	21¼	21¾ in
	48	49	49	50.5	54	54	54	54	55.5 cm
Upper arm	10⅝	12⅜	14½	14½	16⅛	17⅛	18¼	20¼	21⅝ in
	27	31.5	37	37	41	43.5	46.5	51.5	55 cm
Cuff	8½	8½	8⅝	8⅝	9	9½	9⅞	10	10 in
	21.5	21.5	22	22	23.5	24	25	25.5	26 cm
Three-quarter sleeve length from underarm	9⅞	9⅞	9⅞	9⅞	9⅞	9⅞	9⅞	9⅞	9⅞ in
	25	25	25	25	25	25	25	25	25 cm
Full length sleeve from underarm	16½	17	17	17½	17½	18	18	18½	18½ in
	42	43	43	44.5	44.5	45.5	45.5	47	47 cm
Cropped body length from underarm	10	9½	9¼	9	8¾	10	9¼	8¾	8¾ in
	25.5	24	23.5	23	22.5	25.5	23.5	22.5	22.5 cm
Full length body length from underarm	14½	14⅛	14	13½	13⅜	14½	13¾	13½	13⅜ in
	37	36	35.5	34.5	34	37	35	34	34 cm

Hygge jacket

YARN YARDAGE/METERAGE

Amounts include 10% extra for swatching and margin of error.

SIZE	1	2	3	4	5	6	7	8	9
Yarn A	722	820¼	918¾	1061	1236	1400	1553	1728	1925 yd
	660	750	840	970	1130	1280	1420	1580	1760 m
Yarn B	262½	284½	306¼	328¼	372	404¾	437½	459½	481¼ yd
	240	260	280	300	340	370	400	420	440 m
Yarn C	208	229¾	240¾	262½	295½	328¼	350	372	383 yd
	190	210	220	240	270	300	320	340	350 m

FINISHED SIZES

Body length is adjustable to taste.

Designed with 3–5in (8–12.5cm) of positive ease.

SIZE	1	2	3	4	5	6	7	8	9
Bust	32¼	37½	40⅝	44⅜	49⅝	53¼	56⅜	60	65¼ in
	82	95.25	103.25	112.75	126	135.25	143.25	152.75	166 cm
Neck width w/o ribbing	4¼	5¼	7⅜	6¾	7⅞	7⅞	8⅞	8⅞	10½ in
	10.75	13.25	18.75	17.25	20	20	22.75	22.75	26.75 cm
Neck depth w/o ribbing	5¼	6¼	5¾	7⅜	9¼	9¼	8	7⅞	9¾ in
	13.25	16	14.5	18.75	23.5	23.5	20.5	20	24.75 cm
Sleeve circumference	14⅛	14⅛	14⅛	15¾	17¼	19⅜	21	22½	22½ in
	36	36	36	40	44	49.25	53.25	57.25	57.25 cm
Sleeve length from underarm	13½	13½	13½	13½	13½	13½	13½	13½	13½ in
	34.5	34.5	34.5	34.5	34.5	34.5	34.5	34.5	34.5 cm
Body length from underarm	7¾	7¾	7¾	7¾	7¾	7¾	7¾	7¾	7¾ in
	19.5	19.5	19.5	19.5	19.5	19.5	19.5	19.5	19.5 cm

Fernweh tank top

YARN YARDAGE/METERAGE

Amounts include 10% extra for swatching and margin of error.

Amounts are approximate for a cropped top of minimum length as shown on the schematic.

SIZE	1	2	3	4	5	6	7	8	9
Yarn A	197	328¼	372	415¾	601½	656¼	716½	968	1044½ yd
	180	300	340	380	550	600	655	885	955 m
Yarn B	197	328¼	372	415¾	601½	656¼	716½	968	1044½ yd
	180	300	340	380	550	600	655	885	955 m
Yarn C	22	22	22	22	22	22	22	22	22 yd
	20	20	20	20	20	20	20	20	20 m

FINISHED SIZES

Body length is adjustable to desired length.

Designed with 0–2in (0–5cm) of positive ease.

SIZE	1	2	3	4	5	6	7	8	9
Bust	29⅜	32¾	37¼	41½	45	49⅜	53¾	58	62½ in
	74.5	83.25	94.5	105.5	114.5	125.5	136.5	147.5	159 cm
Shoulders	11½	12	13½	14½	14¾	15⅛	15⅛	15¾	15¾ in
	29	30.5	34.25	37	37.5	38.5	38.5	40	40 cm
Armhole depth	7½	7⅞	8⅝	8⅝	9½	9⅞	10⅝	11	11½ in
	19	20	22	22	24	25	27	28	29 cm
Neckline depth	6	6¼	6⅞	6⅞	6⅞	6⅞	7¼	7¼	7¼ in
	15	16	17.5	17.5	17.5	17.5	18.5	18.5	18.5 cm
Minimum length from underarm	5	8⅛	8⅛	8⅛	10½	10⅛	9⅞	12½	12⅛ in
	12.5	20.75	20.75	20.75	26.75	25.75	25	31.75	30.75 cm

Lagom pullover

YARN YARDAGE/METERAGE

Amounts include 10% extra for swatching and margin of error.

Amounts are approximate for a semi-cropped pullover with long sleeves.

SIZE	1	2	3	4	5	6	7	8	9
Yarn A	146¾	163¼	181½	202½	221¾	246½	263½	287¾	304 yd
	134.2	149.2	166	185.2	202.8	225.3	240.8	263	278 m
Yarn B	115	127¾	142	158½	173¾	183	206¼	225	238 yd
	105	116.8	129.9	144.9	158.7	176.3	188.5	205.8	217.6 m
Yarn C	108½	120½	134	149¾	164	182	194¾	212½	224¾ yd
	99.1	110.2	122.6	136.8	149.8	166.4	177.9	194.3	205.4 m
Yarn D	146¾	163¼	181½	202½	222	246½	263½	287¾	304 yd
	134.2	149.2	166	185.2	202.8	225.3	240.8	263	278 m
Yarn E	919	1021½	1136¾	1268	1388¼	1542¾	1649	1801	1903¾ yd
	840.4	934.1	1039.4	1159.5	1269.4	1410.6	1507.9	1646.7	1740.7 m

FINISHED SIZES

Designed with 1–4in (2.5–10cm) of positive ease.

SIZE	1	2	3	4	5	6	7	8	9
Bust	32	35½	39½	42¾	46¾	51¼	54½	57⅞	62 in
	81.5	90	100	108.6	118.5	130	138.5	147	157 cm
Neck	16¾	17¾	20	21¼	23½	24½	25¾	26¼	27½ in
	42.5	45	51	54	59.5	62.5	65	66.5	69.5 cm
Upper arm	11½	11¾	12¾	14	15	16½	17¾	18¾	19⅛ in
	29	30	32.5	35.5	38	42	45	47.5	48.5 cm
Cuff	8¾	8¾	9⅞	10	11¼	11¼	12	12¼	13⅛ in
	22.5	22.5	25	25.5	28.5	28.5	30.5	32.5	33.5 cm
Underarm sleeve length	16½	17	17	17½	17½	18	18	18½	18½ in
	42	43	43	44.5	44.5	45.5	45.5	47	47 cm
Length from underarm	11½	10⅝	10¼	9⅝	8¾	8½	7½	7½	6⅝ in
	29	27	26	24.5	22.5	21.5	19	19	17 cm

Merak hat and cowl

YARN YARDAGE/METERAGE

Amounts include 10% extra for swatching and margin of error.

SIZE	HAT		COWL	
			S	M
Yarn A	153¼		197	295½ yd
	140		180	270 m
Yarn B	54¾		71¼	104 yd
	50		65	95 m
Yarn C	54¾		71¼	104 yd
	50		65	95 m

FINISHED SIZES

Length is adjustable to taste.

SIZE	HAT		COWL	
			S	M
Circumference	21½		23¼	26 in
	54.75		59	66 cm
Length	8¾		11¾	15¾ in
	22.5		30	40 cm

Gigil cardigan

YARN YARDAGE/METERAGE

Amounts include 10% extra for swatching and margin of error.

SIZE	1	2	3	4	5	6	7	8	9
Yarn A	1099¼	1244½	1393½	1567¼	1746½	1925	2097¾	2362¼	2493½ yd
	1005	1138	1274	1433	1597	1760	1918	2160	2280 m
Yarn B	87½	98½	109½	120¼	131¼	142¼	153¼	164¼	175 yd
	80	90	100	110	120	130	140	150	160 m

For the intarsia circles (all sizes)

Yarn B	28½ yd
	26 m
Yarn C	70 yd
	64 m
Yarn D	70 yd
	64 m
Yarn E	50½ yd
	46 m
Yarn F	50½ yd
	46 m
Yarn G	48¼ yd
	44 m
Yarn H	19¾ yd
	18 m
Yarn I	39½ yd
	36 m
Yarn J	28½ yd
	26 m

FINISHED SIZES

Body length is adjustable to desired length.

Designed with 2–5in (5–12.5cm) of positive ease.

SIZE	1	2	3	4	5	6	7	8	9
Bust	33	37	40⅞	44¾	48¾	51⅝	55⅝	59½	64⅜ in
	83.75	93.75	103.75	113.75	123.75	131.25	141.25	151.25	163.75 cm
Neck width	5¾	6	6½	6⅞	7	7¼	7¼	7⅜	7⅜ in
	14.5	15	16.5	17.5	18	18.5	18.5	18.75	18.75 cm
Neck depth	8⅜	8⅜	8¾	8⅜	8¾	8¾	8¾	8¾	9¼ in
	21.25	21.25	22.5	21.25	22.5	22.5	22.5	22.5	23.5 cm
Upper arm	11¾	12¼	13	14	15½	17½	19	20½	21½ in
	30	31	33	35.5	39.5	44.5	48	52	54.75 cm
Cuff	8⅝	8⅝	9	9	9⅝	9⅝	10	10⅝	10⅝ in
	22	22	23	23	24.5	24.5	25.5	27	27 cm
Sleeve length from underarm	17¼	17¾	17¾	18¼	18¼	18¾	18¾	19¼	19¼ in
	44	45	45	46.5	46.5	47.5	47.5	49	49 cm
Body length from underarm	29½	29½	29½	29½	29½	29½	29½	29½	29½ in
	75	75	75	75	75	75	75	75	75 cm

FRONT PANEL PROGRESS TABLE

This table shows what to do on each row of the Front Panels. Use it as support in conjunction to the written instructions.

SIZE	ROWS BEFORE POCKET	POCKET ROWS W/O SHOULDER SHAPING	POCKET ROWS WITH SHOULDER SHAPING	TOTAL POCKET ROWS	ROW COUNT AFTER POCKET	ROWS AFTER POCKET WITH NECK SHAPING	TOTAL ROWS
1	6	11	10	21	27	4	31
2	8	13	8	21	29	6	35
3	10	13	10	23	33	6	39
4	10	17	8	25	35	8	43
5	12	19	6	25	37	10	47
6	14	19	6	25	39	10	49
7	18	19	6	25	43	10	53
8	22	19	6	25	47	10	57
9	28	17	8	25	53	10	63

Pana Po'o summer top

YARN YARDAGE/METERAGE

Amounts include 10% extra for swatching and margin of error.

SIZE	1	2	3	4	5	6	7	8	9
Yarn A	153¼	169½	191½	208	232	246	262½	284½	306¼ yd
	140	155	175	190	212	225	240	260	280 m
Yarn B	175	196	221	238½	268	284½	303	328	354½ yd
	160	179	202	218	245	260	277	300	324 m
Yarn C	174	192½	218¾	235¼	262½	279	300¾	328	350 yd
	159	176	200	215	240	255	275	300	320 m
Yarn D	181½	202½	228¾	247¼	276¾	295½	315	339	366½ yd
	166	185	209	226	253	270	288	310	335 m

FINISHED SIZES

Designed with 1–2⅜in (2.5–6cm) of positive ease.

SIZE	1	2	3	4	5	6	7	8	9
Bust	31	34¼	39	42¼	46¾	50	53½	57⅞	62½ in
	78.6	87	98.6	107	118.5	127	135.7	147	158.6 cm
Neck width	10⅜	10⅜	10⅜	10⅜	10⅜	10⅜	10⅜	10⅜	10⅜ in
	26.5	26.5	26.5	26.5	26.5	26.5	26.5	26.5	26.5 cm
Back length from shoulders	21⅝	21⅝	21⅝	21⅝	21⅝	21⅝	21⅝	21⅝	21⅝ in
	55	55	55	55	55	55	55	55	55 cm

Forelsket shawl

YARN YARDAGE/METERAGE

Amounts include 10% extra for swatching and margin of error.

The pattern is designed and laid out with five different colors in mind. However, the shawl can be worked with as many colors as desired.

The best colors for a seamless faded effect are speckled or marbled yarn in which some aspect of one color relates to the next (such as going from mostly green, to green with purple speckles, to mostly purple). Solids are not the most recommended since they will show the striping pattern too clearly.

Yarn A	164¼ yd
	150 m
Yarn B	262½ yd
	240 m
Yarn C	306¼ yd
	280 m
Yarn D	355½ yd
	325 m
Yarn E	350 yd
	320 m

FINISHED SIZES

Wingspan	72½ in
	184 cm
Length	37⅜ in
	95 cm

Jayus cardigan

YARN YARDAGE/METERAGE

Amounts include 10% extra for swatching and margin of error.

SIZE	1	2	3	4	5	6	7	8	9
Yarn A	459½	525	590¾	667¼	743¾	831¼	907¾	1006¼	1093¾ yd
	420	480	540	610	680	760	830	920	1000 m
Yarn B	284½	328¼	361	415¾	459½	514	557¾	623½	678 yd
	260	300	330	380	420	470	510	570	620 m
Yarn C	383	426½	481¼	545	612½	689	743¾	820¼	897 yd
	350	390	440	500	560	630	680	750	820 m
Yarn D	208	240¾	273½	306¼	339	383	415¾	459½	503 yd
	190	220	250	280	310	350	380	420	460 m

FINISHED SIZES

Body length is adjustable to desired length.

Designed with 2–3in (5–8cm) of positive ease.

SIZE	1	2	3	4	5	6	7	8	9
Bust	31¼	35	39	43	47¼	51¼	54¾	59	64 in
	79	89	99	109	120	130	139	150	162.25 cm
Neck width	3¾	4¾	5½	6⅜	7	7¾	8⅛	8⅝	9¾ in
	9.75	12	14	16.25	18	19.5	20.75	22	24.75 cm
Neck depth	5¾	5¼	5¾	6⅝	7⅜	8	8½	9	10¼ in
	14.5	13.25	14.5	17	18.75	20.5	21.5	23	26 cm
Upper arm	11½	12¼	13⅛	14	15¾	17½	18¾	20	21 in
	29	31	33.5	35.5	40	44.5	47.75	51	53.25 cm
Cuff	8¼	8¼	8¾	8¾	9⅛	9⅝	10	10	10⅞ in
	21	21	22.5	22.5	23.25	24.5	25.5	25.5	27.75 cm
Sleeve length from underarm	16½	17	17	17½	17½	18	18	18½	18½ in
	42	43	43	44.5	44.5	45.5	45.5	47	47 cm
Body length from underarm front	20	20	20	20	20	20	20	20	20 in
	51	51	51	51	51	51	51	51	51 cm
Body length from underarm back	20⅞	20⅞	20⅞	20⅞	20⅞	20⅞	20⅞	20⅞	20⅞ in
	53	53	53	53	53	53	53	53	53 cm

GENERAL TECHNIQUES

Some of the stitches used throughout this book are very simple and straightforward. Others are more modern or are modifications of standard stitches and you might not be familiar with them or with other techniques I encourage you to use. This chapter lists all of these techniques, as well as including other information that you might need to complete the projects in this book. For extra support understanding these techniques, visit NomadStitches.com or head to my Youtube channel at www.youtube.com/c/NomadStitches.

Abbreviations

approx, approximately

beg, beginning

BLO, back loop only

BP, back post

ch(s), chain(s)

ch-sp(s), chain space(s)

cont, continue(d)

csc, central single crochet (waistcoat st)

dc, double crochet

dc2tog, double crochet 2 sts together (dec 1 st): yo, insert hook in first st, yo, pull loop through st (3 loops on hook), yo, pull through 2 loops on hook, yo, insert hook in next st, yo, pull through st (4 loops on hook), yo, pull through 2 loops on hook, yo, pull through rem 3 loops on hook

dcFLO, double crochet worked in the front loop only of stitch 2 rows down for single-row mosaic crochet

dslst, double slip stitch: yo, insert hook in st, yo, pull through st and both loops on hook

dslstBLO, double slip stitch worked through the back loop only

dslstBLO2tog, dslst 2 stitches together through back loops: yo, insert hook in BLO of next st, yo, pull loop through, insert hook in BLO of next st, yo, pull through st and 3 loops on hook

dslstFLO, double slip stitch worked through the front loop only

esc, extended single crochet

FP, front post

FLO, front loop only

foll, follow(ing)

hdc, half double crochet

hdc2tog, half double crochet 2 sts together (dec 1 st): yo, insert hook in first st, yo, pull through st (3 loops on hook), yo, insert hook in next st, yo, pull loop through st (5 loops on hook), yo, pull through all 5 loops on hook

inc1, increase by making 2 sts in the next st

inc2, increase by making 3 sts in the next st

incl, including

mdc mosaic double crochet worked in the skipped st of same color 2 rows down, working in front of intervening rows of ch in other color, for standard mosaic crochet

patt, pattern

PM, place marker

rep, repeat

RS, right side

rsc, reverse single crochet (crab st)

sc, single crochet

sc2tog, single crochet 2 sts together (dec 1 st): [insert hook in next st, yo, pull loop through] twice, yo, pull through all 3 loops on hook

scBLO, single crochet worked through the back loop only

skip, miss

slst, slip stitch

slstBLO, single slip stitch worked through the back loop only

sp(s), space(s)

st(s), stitch(es)

tog, together

WS, wrong side

yo, yarn over hook

All the patterns in this book use repeated sections of instructions to produce the geometric patterns. Repeated sequences are indicated as follows:

......; rep from * to *, work instructions from * to ; and then repeat section between asterisks up to the point specified

*.......; rep from * once more/ twice more/3 times more, work the instructions from * to ; and then repeat that section the number of times specified

[........] once/twice/3 times, work the instructions between the square brackets the total number of times specified

US/UK TERMINOLOGY

All the patterns in this book are written using US crochet terms. See the table below for the equivalent UK stitch names.

US TERM	UK TERM
single crochet	double crochet
half double crochet	half treble crochet
double crochet	treble crochet
yarn over hook	yarn round hook

Basic stitches and techniques

SINGLE CROCHET (SC)

Insert the hook in the stitch, yo, pull through the stitch (1), yo, pull through both loops on the hook. (2)

HALF DOUBLE CROCHET (HDC)

Yo, insert the hook in the stitch (3), yo, pull through the stitch (3 loops on hook), yo, pull through 3 loops on the hook. (4)

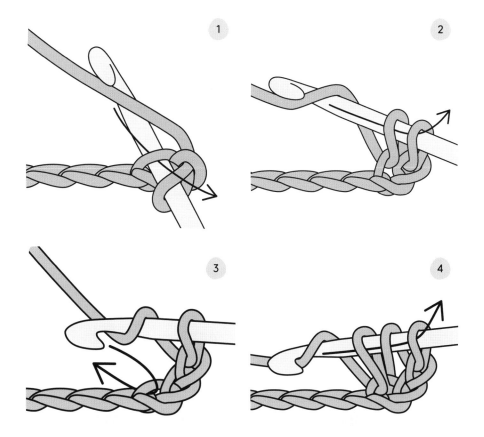

DOUBLE CROCHET (DC)

Yo, insert the hook in the stitch (5), yo, pull through the stitch (3 loops on hook) (6), yo, pull through first 2 loops on the hook, yo, pull through remaining 2 loops on the hook. (7)

REVERSE SINGLE CROCHET (RSC)

Also known as crab stitch. Beginning on the left-hand end of the work, make 1 ch, *insert the hook in the next stitch to the right (8), yo and pull through the stitch keeping the new loop on the hook to left of the one already there (so closer to tip of hook), yo with the working yarn and pull through two loops on the hook (9); rep from * until before last st of row, slst in last stitch of the row.

CENTRAL SINGLE CROCHET (CSC)

Also known as waistcoat stitch. Insert your hook into the center of the V under the top loop, then complete the single crochet in the usual way. (10)

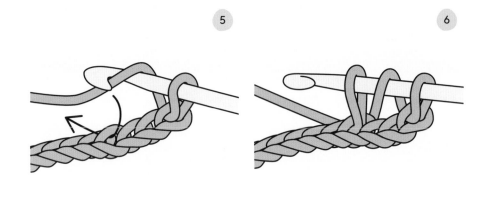

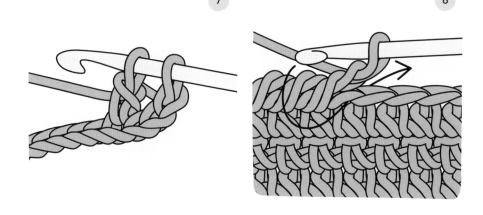

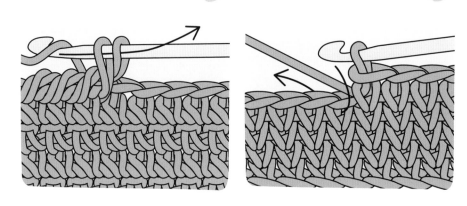

EXTENDED SINGLE CROCHET (ESC)

An extended single crochet is very similar to a regular single crochet: you insert the hook in the next st (under the two loops as normal), yo and pull through the stitch, yo, pull through one loop on the hook (11), yo, and pull through the remaining loops. (12)

WORKING INTO FRONT OR BACK LOOP

Normally you insert the hook into the stitch under both loops at the top. If instructed to work into the front loop only (FLO), work into the loop at the front. (13) If instructed to work into the back loop only (BLO), work into the loop at the back. (14)

BACK POST SINGLE CROCHET (BPSC)

This stitch is worked around the post of a stitch instead on the top loops like usual. Insert the hook from back to front before the post of the stitch below, then bring it from front to back again (15), yarn over and pull through around the post of the stitch, yo, pull through all loops on the hook. (16)

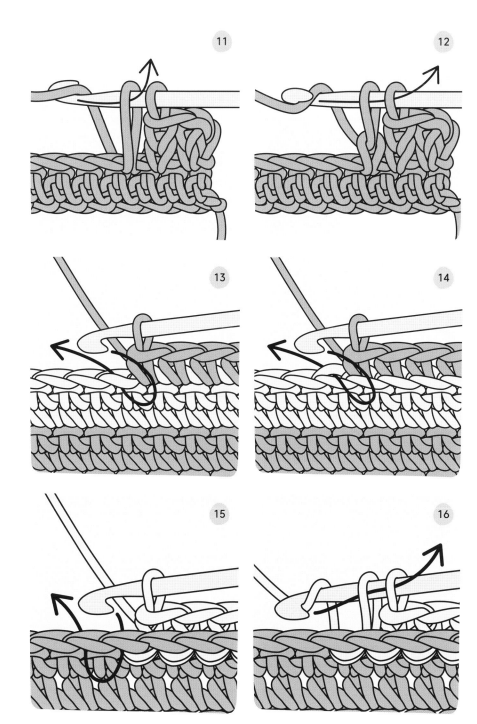

CROCHET CORD

This technique is a tidy alternative to a starting chain at the beginning of your work. Work cord stitches loosely to avoid a tight edge. Leaving a tail of about 2.5 times the desired length of the cord, make a slip knot and place it on the hook. *From front to back, wrap the tail around the hook, yo with the working yarn (17), pull through the 2 loops on your hook (slip knot and tail) (18); rep from * until required number of stitches have been created. (19)

Changing color

On the last stitch of the first color, wrap the tail around the hook, pick up the new color and pull through both loops on the hook (20), leaving a tail to continue working the cord with the new color. (21)

FAUX I-CORD EDGING

This edging emulates a knitted i-cord and can be done at the beginning or end of a project worked in the round.

To work at the beginning: make a chain as long as the edging, slip stitch in the first chain to join and work a round of single crochet. Do not join but continue in a spiral, [back post single crochet around, PM to denote beg of round] 3 or more times. Join the last round to the starting chain by working single crochet back loop only around stitches on the last round and the unused loops of the starting chain, slip stitch in the first stitch to join— the last row marks the RS.

To work at the end: single crochet around, do not join but continue in a spiral, [back post single crochet around, PM to denote beg of round] 3 or more times. Leave as is, or make it more "tube-like" by fastening off, leaving a long tail at least twice the circumference of your work, then sewing the back loop of stitches on the last round onto the back of the first round of edging without going through to the right side of the work.

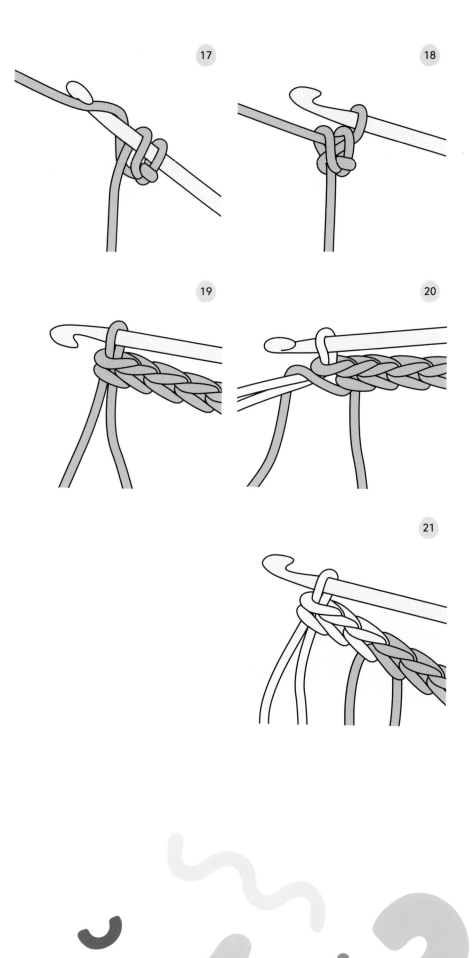

INVISIBLE JOIN WHEN WORKING IN ROUNDS

Make a slip stitch in the first stitch to join the round (22), then pull to tighten the slip stitch (23), 1 ch (which does not count as a stitch) and pull to tighten the chain (24). If the turning chain calls for more than 1 chain, then work the following chain counting the tightened chain as the first one.

INVISIBLE JOIN TO FASTEN OFF WHEN WORKING IN ROUNDS

After finishing the last stitch of the round, cut the yarn leaving a tail and pull it through the stitch. Thread the tail into a tapestry needle, insert the needle under both loops of the second stitch of the round (25) and pull through, then insert needle into last stitch of the round in between the top loops (26). Pull through and adjust the loop created to imitate the look of a stitch, then fasten off on the inside and weave in the end.

MATTRESS STITCH

Align the two pieces to be joined next to each other. Pass a threaded tapestry needle from back to front where the seam is to start on one piece. Pull through the stitch, then rep on the other piece, passing the needle from back to front. Continue alternating from one piece to the other and threading through every stitch, making sure that your tension is even.

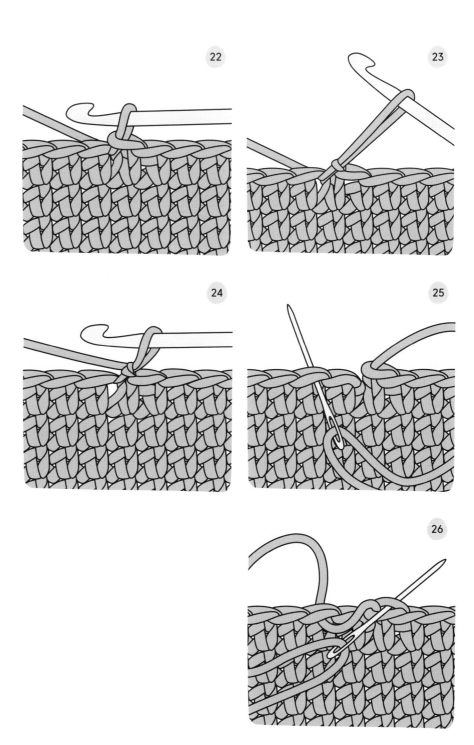

About the Author

Sandra was born and raised in Mexico. After graduating with a Psychology degree from a university in the US, she went on to teach English as a second language. This allowed her to travel and live in different places around the world, learning from, and being inspired by, new cultures. She started designing knitwear professionally in 2016 while living in Spain, but didn't start doing it full-time until the birth of her first daughter in 2019 while living in Bulgaria. She now lives in the UK with her husband, two daughters and two dogs. You can find her designs as Nomad Stitches on Ravelry or NomadStitches.com.

Suppliers

Retrosaria Rosa Pomar
retrosaria.rosapomar.com

KnitPicks
www.knitpicks.com

WeCrochet
www.crochet.com

Less Traveled Yarn
travelingyarn.com

The Fibre Co
thefibreco.com

Spincycle Yarns
spincycleyarns.com

Sirdar Yarn
sirdar.com

La Bien Aimee
www.labienaimee.com

Lovecrafts
www.lovecrafts.com

Acknowledgments

Writing this book and creating all of the designs has been much more challenging and rewarding than I ever imagined it would be. And I certainly couldn't have done it alone!

First of all, I have to thank my loving husband, Calum, who picked up my slack around the home to care for me and our daughter Magnolia. Thank you also for being my best critic. None of this would be possible without you.

I am forever grateful to my mom and dad for teaching me to love working with my hands and to believe in myself.

I also have to thank my mother-in-law, Sabrina, and her husband, Phil for providing studio space at a heavily discounted rate!

A big thanks to the team at David and Charles, who worked tirelessly on the publishing side, and a special note to Marie Clayton, who was ever so patient with my never-ending questions and edits.

On that note, I must thank Jemima Bicknell, my tech editor and maths genius who went over the patterns with a fine-tooth comb. And I can't leave out my lovely testers whose feedback and tireless work made these patterns the best they could be.

Last, but not least, a massive thanks to the wonderful companies who provided yarn support and who made this book a truly international cooperation: from Sirdar Yarns, The Fibre Co, Love Crafts, and Knit Picks in the UK, to La Rosa Pomar in Portugal, La Bien Aimee in France, and all the way to Less Traveled Yarn and Spincycle Yarns in the US. Thank you all!

I hope you have enjoyed learning the techniques which I so love, and that you have found joy in the patterns provided in this book. Thanks to all of my readers for supporting my work.

INDEX

This book has been printed on paper from approved
suppliers and made from pulp from sustainable
sources.

Printed in the UK by Page Bros for:
David and Charles, Ltd
Suite A, Tourism House, Pynes Hill, Exeter, EX2 5WS

10 9 8 7 6 5 4 3 2 1

Publishing Director: Ame Verso
Senior Commissioning Editor: Sarah Callard
Managing Editor: Jeni Chown
Project Editor: Marie Clayton
Head of Design: Sam Staddon
Designer: Lucy Waldron
Pre-press Designer: Ali Stark
Illustrations: Kuo Kang Chen
Art Direction: Sarah Rowntree
Photography: Jason Jenkins
Production Manager: Beverley Richardson

David and Charles publishes high-quality books on
a wide range of subjects. For more information visit
www.davidandcharles.com.

Share your makes with us on social media using
#dandcbooks and follow us on Facebook and
Instagram by searching for @dandcbooks.

Layout of the digital edition of this book may vary
depending on reader hardware and display settings.